WORKBOO

BIG
ENGLISH 5

Mario Herrera • **Christopher Sol Cruz**

Big English
Workbook 5

Pearson Education, 10 Bank Street, White Plains, NY 10606 USA

Staff credits: The people who made up the *Big English* team, representing editorial, production, design, manufacturing, and marketing are Rhea Banker, Danielle Belfiore, Carol Brown, Tracey Munz Cataldo, Daniel Comstock, Mindy DePalma, Dave Dickey, Gina DiLillo, Christine Edmonds, Nancy Flaggman, Yoko Mia Hirano, Caroline Kasterine, Amy Kefauver, Lucille Kennedy, Penny Laporte, Christopher Leonowicz, Emily Lippincott, Maria Pia Marrella, Jennifer McAliney, Kate McLoughlin, Julie Molnar, Linda Moser, Kyoko Oinuma, Leslie Patterson, Sherri Pemberton, Pamela Pia, Stella Reilly, Nicole Santos, Susan Saslow, Donna Schaffer, Chris Siley, Kim Snyder, Heather St. Clair, Mairead Stack, Katherine Sullivan, Jane Townsend, Kenneth Volcjak, and Lauren Weidenman.

Contributing Writer: Teresa Lintner

Text composition: Bill Smith Group/Q2A Media

Illustration credits: Q2A Media Services, Anthony Lewis

Photo credits: Title/Cover (bc) Monkey Business/Fotolia; 2 (tl) Ingram Publishing/Thinkstock, (tc) Mira/Alamy, (tr) prudkov/Shutterstock, (cl) Darrin Henry/Fotolia, (c) paul abbitt rml/Alamy, (cr) auremar/Shutterstock; 3 (c) Ulrich Doering/Glow Images; 4 (tl) Dhoxax/Shutterstock, (tr) Jörg Hackemann/Fotolia, (cr) David Davis/Shutterstock; 8 (tl) Jim Cummins/CORBIS/Glow Images, (tr) Monkey Business/Fotolia; 9 (tl) Simon Balson/Alamy; 10 (bcr) Paul B. Moore/Shutterstock; 11 (c) Amos Morgan/Photodisc/Getty Images, (cr) Dan Thornberg/Shutterstock, (bc) KidStock/Blend Images/Getty Images, (bcr) Hywit Dimyadi/Shutterstock, (b) Radius Images/Glow Images, (br) Ulrich Doering/Glow Images; 12 (tl) Andres Rodriguez/Fotolia, (tc) Westend61/Getty Images, (tr) Stockbyte/Getty Images, (cl) Jupiterimages/Getty Images, (c) Kim Ruoff/Shutterstock; 15 (tr boy) Hitoshi Nishimura/Getty Images, (tr girl) Stock4B/Getty Images; 18 (tr) Jeffery Drewitz/Cephas Picture Library/Alamy, (tcl) Dimijian Greg/Getty Images, (cr) De Agostini Picture Library/Getty Images, 19 (tl) Irene Abdou/Alamy, (tr) Wallenrock/Shutterstock, (cl) Tim Gainey/Alamy, (cr) Neil Setchfield/Alamy; 20 (tr) Jason Merritt/Getty Images; 22 (tl) Myrleen Pearson/Alamy, (tc) Jim West/Alamy, (tr) ZUMA Wire Service/Alamy, (cl) SelectStock/Getty Images, (c) nagelestock.com/Alamy, (cr) Morgan Lane Photography/Alamy; 29 (tr) Xavier Bonghi/Getty Images, (cr) George Doyle/Thinkstock; 31 (tl) Lev Dolgatsjov/Fotolia, (tr) eurobanks/Shutterstock, (tcl) EJ White/Fotolia, (tcr) Ken Hurst/Fotolia; 32 (karate) paul abbitt rml/Alamy, (painter) Mira/Alamy, (guitarist) Darrin Henry/Fotolia, (actors) Ulrich Doering/Glow Images, (graduation) Andres Rodriguez/Fotolia, (store owners) Jupiterimages/Getty Images, (moving) Westend61/Getty Images, (wedding) Stockbyte/Getty Images, (bake sale) ZUMA Wire Service/Alamy, (reading) Myrleen Pearson/Alamy, (digging) Jim West/Alamy, (recycling) Morgan Lane Photography/Alamy; 34 (tl) Pumba/Fotolia, (tc) Konstantin Yolshin/Fotolia, (tr) nobleIMAGES/Alamy, (cl) Fotomatador/Alamy, (c) Ferenc Szelepcsenyi/Shutterstock, (cr) Allstar Picture Library/Alamy; 36 (tl) Oleksiy Maksymenko/Glowimages; 37 (tr) Tomasz Trojanowski/Shutterstock; 38 (bkgd) Barauskaite/Shutterstock; 40 (cr) for you design/Shutterstock; 41 (tr) Thailand/Alamy, (cr) Travelasia/Getty Images; 42 (tr) marekuliasz/Shutterstock; 43 (cl) 2tun/Fotolia, (c) Zedcor Wholly Owned/Thinkstock, (cr) Bombaert Patrick/Shutterstock; 44 (tl) Purestock/Thinkstock, (tc) Monkey Business/Thinkstock, (tr) Image Source/Corbis, (cl) Kuttig-Travel/Alamy, (c) Tan Kian Khoon/Fotolia, (cr) Purestock/Thinkstock; 45 (bl) Ken Hurst/Fotolia; 49 (tl) Mitchell Knapton/Fotolia, (tr) SUSAN LEGGETT/Shutterstock, (cl) baitong333/Shutterstock, (cr) Myrleen Pearson/Alamy, (bl) Monkey Business/Fotolia, (br) Rex Moreton/Bubbles Photolibrary/Alamy; 51 (tr) wavebreakmedia/Shutterstock, (tcr) Delphimages/Fotolia; 52 (cr) Boobl/Shutterstock; 55 (tl) Denys Prykhodov/Fotolia, (tcl) FERNANDO BLANCO CALZADA/Shutterstock, (tcr) plutofrosti/Fotolia, (tr) Igor Klimov/Fotolia; 56 (tr) charles taylor/Shutterstock, (tc) Thibault Renard/Fotolia, (cl) Vladislav Ociacia/Fotolia, (bcr) Vladislav Ociacia/Fotolia; 61 (tr) Owen Franken/Corbis; 63 (tl) eurobanks/Shutterstock, (tc) Zedcor Wholly Owned/Thinkstock, (bracelet) neelsky/Shutterstock, (camera) neelsky/Shutterstock, (headphones) marekuliasz/Shutterstock, (frame) Barbara Helgason/Fotolia, (sunglasses) badmanproduction/Fotolia, (helmet) Ljupco Smokovski/Shutterstock, (bug spray) andrea crisante/Shutterstock, (jacket) Karkas/Shutterstock, (phone) Lifdiz/Shutterstock, (tablet) plutofrosti/Fotolia, (mp3 player) Patrick McCall/Shutterstock, (laptop) Igor Klimov/Fotolia; 66 (tl) Carsten Reisinger/Shutterstock, (tr) Eddows arunothai/Shutterstock, (inset) Stephen VanHorn/Shutterstock, (cl) PRILL/Shutterstock, (cr) Aqua Stock/Shutterstock; 67 (tl) J.C. Towers/Corbis, (tcl) Hemera/Thinkstock, (tcr) arska n/Fotolia, (tr) Rambleon/Shutterstock, (bl) neelsky/Shutterstock, (bcl) TOMOHIRO IWANAGA/a.collectionRF/Getty Images, (bcr) pagadesign/Getty Images, (br) Denys Prykhodov/Shutterstock; 68 (tr) DeSerg/Shutterstock, (bl) Andy Crawford/Dorling Kindersley; 69 (br) Werner Forman Archive/Glow Image; 70 (tl) Nata-Lia/Shutterstock, (cl) djem/Shutterstock, (bcl) Igor Grochev/Shutterstock, (bl) Lithium366/Fotolia; 71 (tl) Science & Society Picture Library/Getty Images, (tcl) Kemeo/Shutterstock, (bcl) Pinosub/Shutterstock, (bl) English School/Getty Images; 72 (tcr) James Clarke/Shutterstock, (cr) marykatherinedonovan/Shutterstock, (bcr) Erika Cross/Shutterstock; 73 (tr) higyou/Shutterstock, (c) Vadim Petrakov /Shutterstock, Panu Ruangjan/Shutterstock, (bcr) Photo Japan/Alamy; 75 (bluetooth) Oleksandr Chub /Shutterstock, (camera) neelsky/Shutterstock, (radio) TOMOHIRO IWANAGA/a.collectionRF/Getty Imtextages, (earphones) Nata-Lia/Shutterstock, (shoelaces) djem/Shutterstock, (watch) Igor Grochev/Shutterstock, (controller) Lithium366/Fotolia; 76 (tl) MasterLu/Fotolia, (tr) RuthChoi/Shutterstock, (bl) BGSmith/Shutterstock, (br) Martin M303/Fotolia; 77 (cl) 101imges/Shutterstock, (cr) Melinda Fawver/Shutterstock, (bl) Picsfive/Shutterstock, (br) Yves Forestier/Alamy; 78 (cr) Sean Davey/Getty Images; 81 (child) emese73/Fotolia, (balloons) Douglas Knight/Fotolia, (shopping cart) Cybrain/Fotolia, (gramaphone) dja65/Fotolia, (car) Car Culture/Corbis, (gold) Aaron Amat/Shutterstock, (chess) Steve Smith/Shutterstock, (boots) Milos Tasic/Fotolia; 82 (tr) Nick Turner/Alamy; 83 (tr) Lew Robertson/Corbis, (c) Keith Brofsky/Getty Images; 85 (cr) Vitaly Maksimchuk/Shutterstock; 86 (tl) Christelle/Fotolia, (tc) Joe Gough/Fotolia, (tr) Barnabas Kindersley/DK Images, (c) bonchan/Shutterstock, (cr) dreambigphotos/Fotolia; 87 (guacamole) jreika/Fotolia, (babotie) Ehrman Photographic/Shutterstock, (kimchi) Dream79/Shutterstock, (sashimi) design sweet/Shutterstock, (chicken) Irina Zavyalova/Shutterstock, (grasshopper) Photomorgana/Corbis; 88 (tr) Stephen Frink/Corbis, (cr) Audrey Snider-Bell/Shutterstock; 92 (tr) Zeamonkey Images/Shutterstock, (cr) idp oulton park bike collection/Alamy; 93 (tr) Splash News/Newscom, (cr) MARCEL ANTONISSE/AFP/Getty Images; 99 (tl) BVDC/Fotolia, (tcl) EyeMark/Fotolia; 100 (tl) Mike Flippo/Shutterstock, (tcl) NinaMalyna/Shutterstock, (cl) iofoto/Shutterstock; 103 (tl) Ken Hurst/Fotolia; 105 (tr) Sally Scott/Shutterstock; 107 (bc) Jenkedco/Shutterstock; 108 (tl) Everett Collection Inc/Alamy, (cl) Iveta Angelova/Shutterstock, (cr) Max Topchii/Shutterstock

Printed in the United States of America

ISBN-10: 0-13-304518-8
ISBN-13: 978-0-13-3045185

Contents

BIG ENGLISH

♫ Song ♫

From the mountaintops to the bottom of the sea,
From a big blue whale to a baby bumblebee—
If you're big, if you're small, you can have it all,
And you can be anything you want to be!

It's bigger than you. It's bigger than me.
There's so much to do, and there's so much to see!
The world is big and beautiful, and so are we!
Think big! Dream big! Big English!

So in every land, from the desert to the sea,
We can all join hands and be one big family.
If we love, if we care, we can go anywhere!
The world belongs to everyone; it's ours to share.

It's bigger than you. It's bigger than me.
There's so much to do, and there's so much to see!
The world is big and beautiful, and so are we!
Think big! Dream big! Big English!

It's bigger than you. It's bigger than me.
There's so much to do, and there's so much to see!
The world is big and beautiful and waiting for me . . .
        a one, two, three . . .
Think big! Dream big! Big English!

unit 1 MY INTERESTS

1 Listen to the activities. Which of the activities do you see in the pictures? Write the number.

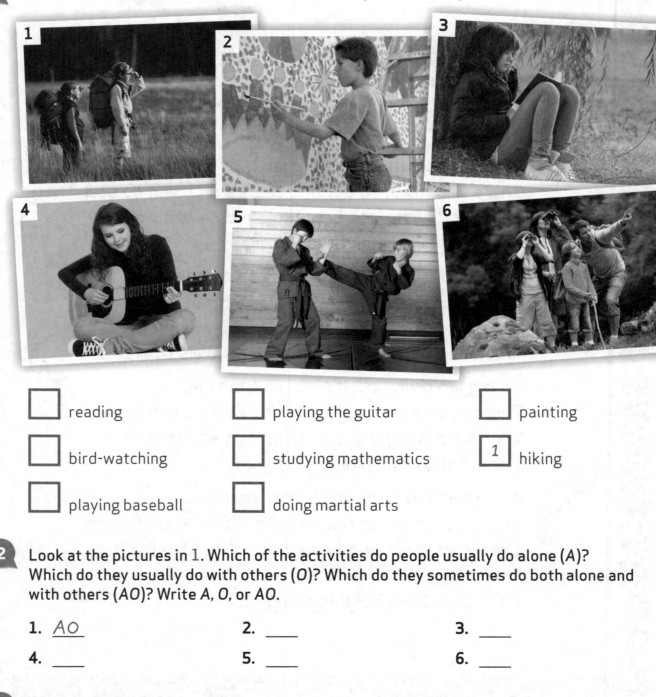

☐ reading	☐ playing the guitar	☐ painting
☐ bird-watching	☐ studying mathematics	1 hiking
☐ playing baseball	☐ doing martial arts	

2 Look at the pictures in 1. Which of the activities do people usually do alone (A)? Which do they usually do with others (O)? Which do they sometimes do both alone and with others (AO)? Write A, O, or AO.

1. _AO_   2. ____   3. ____

4. ____   5. ____   6. ____

3 What activities in 1 do you do in your free time? Write the numbers.

_____

4 Find and circle the six interests. Then write them.

```
      g  t  a
   z  c  p  u  l
   e  c  h (b  a  n  d)
s  c  i  e  n  c  e  o  m
b  b  a  s  e  b  a  l  l
   a  n  s  t  r  a  c  k
   n  d  r  a  m  a
   d  f  i  u
      i  o
```

1. b_and_____
2. d_____
3. t_____
4. b_____
5. c_____
6. s_____

5 Match the interests with the school groups. Write the letter.

Interests

_e_ **1.** martial arts

___ **2.** acting

___ **3.** writing articles

___ **4.** playing music

___ **5.** building things

School Groups

a. drama club

b. science club

c. school band

d. school newspaper

e. tae kwon do club

6 What are you good at? What school group do you want to join? Complete the sentences.

I'm good at _____.

I want to join _____.

 **7** Listen and read. Then answer the questions.

Manhasset School News Opinion Page

| Home | For Staff | For Students | School Directory | Clubs |

DO WHAT'S RIGHT FOR YOU

bbrown

It's a new school year. Everyone is talking about the new after-school clubs because they're fun. You can learn new things and make new friends. But some students aren't interested in joining clubs. They may be shy or scared of groups. These students may be good at singing or playing an instrument, but they like doing these activities alone. They don't want to join clubs, and that's OK.

I'm a shy girl. I enjoy watching sports on TV, painting, and playing my guitar. I'm not interested in joining a sports team, art club, or the school band. My friends were mad at me because I didn't want to join their clubs, so I talked to my mom about it. She said, "It's OK. Be yourself. Do the things you like to do." I want to say to shy kids like me, "Do what is right for you. Find friends who are like you. You don't always have to do what everyone else does."

Comments

Ssilver

I'm a shy kid, too. I always feel bad when my classmates talk about signing up for after-school clubs. I'm glad to know that I'm not the only one.

suki.park

Wow! I love clubs and I never thought some kids didn't want to join them. Thanks for writing this. Personally, I don't like to do things alone, so clubs are good for me.

1. What is this newsletter about?

   _____

2. Is the newsletter writer interested in joining clubs? Why or why not?

   _____

3. What does she enjoy doing?

   _____

4. Is bbrown shy?

   _____

8 What do you think about the newsletter? Add your own comment.

_____

9 Listen. Then read and circle *T* for *True* or *F* for *False*.

Cathy:	Are you interested in joining a club this year, Ben?
Ben:	<u>I don't know</u> . . . I don't have much time. I usually have homework. And when I have free time, I read my manga comics.
Cathy:	Manga? Those Japanese comic books? Cool! Hey, did you hear that there's a manga club at school this year?
Ben:	<u>No way</u>!
Cathy:	Yeah, <u>seriously</u>. You can sign up in Mr. Wang's room.
Ben:	Where did you hear about it? When does it meet?
Cathy:	Kenna told me about it. I joined yesterday! It meets on Wednesdays and Fridays.
Ben:	Oh, good. I can do that.
Cathy:	<u>Great</u>! See you there tomorrow.

1. Ben has a lot of free time.   T   F
2. The manga club meets twice a week.   T   F
3. Ben is going to join the manga club. T   F
4. Cathy hasn't joined the manga club.   T   F

10 Look at 9. Read the underlined expressions. How can you say them in other words? Match and write the letter.

_d_ 1. I don't know.

___ 2. No way!

___ 3. Seriously.

___ 4. Great!

a. This is good news.

b. It's true. It's not a joke!

c. I'm *really* surprised. I can't believe it.

d. I'm not sure what I want to do.

11 Complete the sentences with the expressions in 10. Then listen and check your answers.

A: Our class is going to Disneyland for our class trip.

B: ¹_____! How exciting! When do you leave?

A: Tomorrow morning at 4 AM.

B: ²_____! That's crazy! It's so early!

A: Yeah, ³_____. Four in the morning.

B: How will you wake up that early?

A: ⁴_____. Maybe my mom will wake me up.

| How about **joining** the baseball team? | OK. I <u>love</u> **playing** baseball. |
| How <u>about</u> **trying out** for the school play? | Cool. I'<u>m good at</u> **acting**. |

12 Look at the pictures of Sue and Keenan. Complete the sentences. Use the correct form of the verbs.

> do tae kwon do   play chess   play soccer   take photos

1. Sue and Keenan both enjoy _____.
2. Sue enjoys _____. Keenan isn't interested in it.
3. Sue has a good camera. She likes _____.
4. Keenan enjoys martial arts. He loves _____.

13 Complete the sentences. Circle the correct form of the verbs.

1. **A:** How about **joins** / **joining** the basketball team?

   B: I'm not sure. I'm not very good at **playing** / **play** basketball.

2. **A:** How about **joining** / **you join** the tae kwon do club?

   B: Great! I love **do** / **doing** martial arts.

3. **A:** How about **tries** / **trying** out for the school play?

   B: I don't know. I'm not very interested in **acts** / **acting**.

4. **A:** How about **goes** / **going** to the new action movie with me on Saturday?

   B: Well, maybe. But I don't really like **watching** / **watches** action movies.

14 Write the questions. Use *How about* and the words in the box.

Do you like playing sports? Yes / No
Are you interested in acting? Yes / No
Do you like doing math problems? Yes / No
Do you enjoy writing stories? Yes / No

Nora

> join/science club   join/school news bloggers   audition for /school play   try out for/track team

1. **Paula:** _____
   Nora: Good idea! I really enjoy playing sports.

2. **Paula:** _____
   Nora: I don't know. I'm not good at acting.

3. **Paula:** _____
   Nora: That's a good idea. I'm great at math, and I love doing projects.

4. **Paula:** _____
   Nora: Sounds great! I enjoy writing!

15 Complete the sentences about a friend. Use *he* or *she*.

My friend's name is _____. _____ likes _____, and
_____ is good at _____. _____ isn't interested in
_____, but _____ and I enjoy _____.

16 Read the questions. Write the answer about yourself.

1. How about trying out for the soccer team?

   _____

2. How about joining the book club?

   _____

3. How about joining the science club?

   _____

4. How about auditioning for the school band?

   _____

17 Read. Then circle the correct name.

Left Brained or Right Brained ?

Tom

"I have a left-brained personality. I'm really good at solving math problems, and I like working alone. I enjoy writing, but I'm not good at being creative. I'm very organized. In class I like listening and taking notes. I usually remember the details when I read. When I study, I write things down and make lists. They help me remember."

Sara

"Honestly, I'm the opposite of Tom. I'm very creative. I love drawing and playing music. I enjoy working in groups and solving problems together. I like surprises, but I'm not any good at organizing things. Sometimes I talk when I shouldn't, and I get distracted when I should be listening. When I study, I draw pictures because it helps me remember."

1. Who likes doing projects in groups?   Tom   Sara
2. Who should be a member of the drama club?   Tom   Sara
3. Who should be a School News blogger?   Tom   Sara
4. Who is probably quieter in class?   Tom   Sara

18 Match the words with the definitions. Write the letter.

___ 1. personality   **a.** good at thinking of new ideas

___ 2. brain   **b.** the unique combination of traits that characterize a person

___ 3. control   **c.** the part of your body that controls how you think, feel, and move

___ 4. instructions   **d.** find the answer to a problem

___ 5. solve   **e.** information telling you how to do something

___ 6. creative   **f.** make someone or something do what you want

19 Complete the sentences. Use words in **18**.

1. The _____ has two sides—left and right.

2. Each side of our brain controls different parts of our _____.

3. Can you _____ math problems easily? You might be left brained.

4. Do you enjoy being _____? Then you might be right brained.

20 Read. Then rewrite the sentences so that they are true.

Cool Olympic Sport

Do you like riding your bike fast? Did you know that extra-fast bike riding is a sport at the Olympics? Bike racing started as an Olympic sport in Athens in 1896. Over the years, there were road races and track races and mountain-bike racing in the Olympic Games. Then, in the 2008 Beijing Games, a bike sport called BMX became a new Olympic sport. BMX started in California around 1968. It's a very fast and dangerous sport, so competitors have to be fearless to take part!

Both men and women compete in BMX. The bikes are light and very strong. They need to be strong enough for all the jumps and ramps and yet remain light, so the riders can travel as fast as possible. The tracks for men are about 450m long. They are a little shorter for women. But all the races last only 40 seconds! If you blink, you'll miss them!

The riders have created new words to talk about their sport, such as bunny-hop. A bunny-hop is when a rider's bike goes up in the air. The riders in the picture are bunny-hopping. Another word is whoop. A whoop is a small bump in the road. The next time you ride your bike, look out for whoops and don't bunny-hop. Stay safe!

1. Only men compete in BMX. _____

2. The bikes are heavy. _____

3. The race lasts 60 seconds. _____

4. A bunny-hop is a small bump in the road. _____

21 Find these numbers in the reading in 20. Write the sentences with these numbers.

1. nineteen sixty-eight

   BMX started in California around 1968.

2. two thousand and eight

   _____

3. four hundred and fifty

   _____

4. eighteen ninety-six

   _____

22 Answer the question.

Would you like to watch a BMX race? Why or why not?

_____

A good news article includes important information about an event. It includes the answers to these questions: *Who* is the article about? *What* is the article about? *When* did the event happen? *Where* did the event happen? *What happened?*

A good news article also gives other information to make the story interesting, but don't forget to answer the questions!

KEY QUESTIONS:
Who?
What?
When?
Where?
What happened?

23 Read the answers (A). Complete the questions (Q) with *Who, What, When, Where,* or *What happened.*

1. **Q:** _____? You're all dirty!

   A: I slipped and fell in the mud outside school!

2. **Q:** _____ is that over there?

   A: That's my science club leader.

3. **Q:** _____ do you do in science club?

   A: We play chess and other fun games.

4. **Q:** _____ does the club meet?

   A: It meets in the science lab.

5. **Q:** _____ does your science club meet?

   A: It meets on Mondays after school.

24 Write a news article on a separate piece of paper. Use the information in the chart. Add interesting information.

Who?	What ?	
People who enjoy acting	Audition for the musical *Peter Pan*	
When?	**Where?**	**What happened?**
Last Monday after school	In the auditorium	More than twenty students auditioned for the lead roles
Interesting Information:		
Everyone was nervous. Mr. Bannister is going to post the results on the school website. Good luck to all who auditioned!		

Peter Pan

25 Where do these activities <u>usually</u> take pace? Write the words in the correct column.

> act on stage   march in a band   play baseball
> play the piano   play soccer   write articles

Inside	Outside
_____	_____
_____	_____
_____	_____
_____	_____

26 Write questions with *how about* and the words in parentheses.
Then look at the picture and complete the answers.

1. **Peggy:** Carla, _____
   _____?
   (try out for/soccer team)
   Carla: No way! You know I only play
   _____.

2. **James:** Olivia, _____
   _____?
   (sign up for/school newspaper)
   Olivia: Great idea! I really enjoy
   _____.

3. **Marco:** _____
   _____?
   (join/the marching band)
   Daniel: No, I can't play an instrument, but I'm
   interested in _____.
   Maybe I'll join the drama club.

unit 2 FAMILY TIES

1 Match the pictures and the sentences. Write the number.

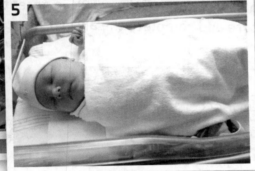

☐ The couple got married.

☐ The family moved to a new house.

☐ The baby was born at 5 AM.

☐ The students graduated from college.

☐ The family opened a store.

2 Answer the questions about your family. Circle *Yes* or *No*.

In the last four years:

		Yes	No
1.	Did your family open a store?	Yes	No
2.	Did you move to a new home?	Yes	No
3.	Did a family member graduate from a school?	Yes	No
4.	Was a new family member born?	Yes	No
5.	Did a family member get married?	Yes	No

3 Match and complete the phrases. Write the number.

1. graduated
2. moved
3. got
4. opened
5. was

a. ___ to a new place
b. ___ from business school
c. ___ born
d. ___ a store
e. ___ married

 4 Look at the timeline of Ken's life. Listen to the events. Then write the events.

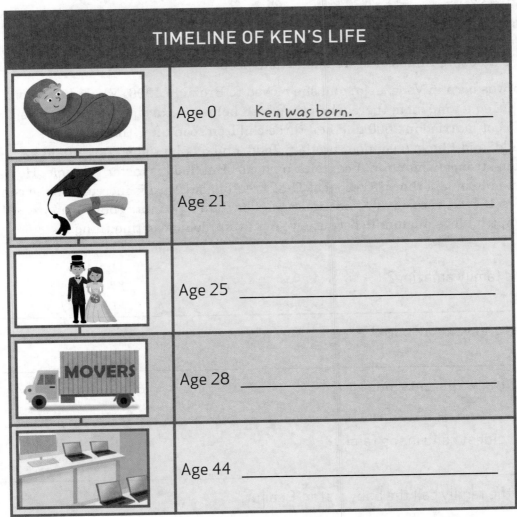

TIMELINE OF KEN'S LIFE

	Age 0 Ken was born.
	Age 21 _____
	Age 25 _____
	Age 28 _____
	Age 44 _____

5 Write the words for these family members. Use *aunt*, *brother*, *sister*, or *uncle*.

1. My mom's sister is my _____.
2. My dad's brother is my _____.
3. My aunt is my dad's _____.
4. My uncle is my mom's _____.

6 Listen and read. Then answer the questions.

My Amazing Family

My name is Tracy, and I have an unusual and amazing family. We're superheroes! We can do amazing things, and we like to help people.

My mom was born in Venezuela, and she moved to Brazil in 1996. My dad was born in Brazil. He met my mom there when they both helped to save people in a house fire. They got married in 2000 and had three children soon after that. I am the oldest child, and I have a younger brother, Todd, and a baby sister, Tara. Todd is eight. I am stronger than him. I can pick up a car! But Todd is faster than me. He can run a mile in less than 15 seconds! That's really fast! Tara is incredible! She can make herself very, very small, sometimes smaller than a peanut. That's why we call her "Peanut." I love my family because we're always doing exciting things.

1. Why is this family amazing?

   _____

2. Where was Tracy's mom born?

   _____

3. Where did Tracy's parents meet?

   _____

4. Who is the oldest child in the family?

   _____

5. Why does the family call the baby sister "Peanut?"

   _____

7 Answer the questions.

1. Which power would you like to have? Why?

   _____

2. What are you going to do with that power?

   _____

8 Listen. Then circle the correct answers.

Wayne: Oh... this is a great picture! What a cute baby!

Deb: Guess who...?

Wayne: No! That's not you! Is it?

Deb: Yeah... that's me. That's the day I was born.

Wayne: Really? But... what happened?

Deb: What do you mean?

Wayne: You were so much cuter then!

Deb: Ha! Ha! Very funny. My mother says I was the cutest baby in the world.

Wayne: Well, I don't know... But you were pretty cute.

Deb: Thanks.

1. Who is the baby in the picture?

    a. someone in Wayne's family   **b.** Deb

2. Wayne ___ when he says that Deb was cuter when she was a baby.

    a. is serious   **b.** is joking

3. Deb's mom said that she was the cutest baby in the world. Wayne ___.

    a. agrees   **b.** doesn't really agree

9 Look at 8. Read the underlined expressions. How can you say them in other words? Match and write the letter.

___ **1.** Really?

___ **2.** What do you mean?

___ **3.** Ha! Ha! Very funny.

___ **4.** Well, I don't know...

a. I don't understand what you are talking about.

b. That's not funny.

c. I don't think that's exactly true.

d. I am very surprised.

10 Circle the correct expression.

1. **A:** That's a picture of my brother.

    B: Really? / Ha! Ha! Very funny. You don't look like him at all.

    A: But we're twins!

2. **A:** That's the day we moved.

    B: What do you mean? / Well, I don't know.

    A: We moved from New York to Ohio.

    B: I didn't know that!

Grammar

We **went** to Los Angeles <u>when</u> I **was** eight.
<u>When</u> they **were** kids, they **lived** in Mexico City.

She **moved** to Florida three years <u>ago</u>.
A few months <u>later</u>, she **got** a new job.

11 **Find and circle each past tense verb. There are ten verbs.**

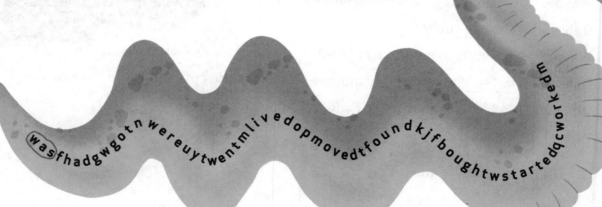

~~was~~fhadgwgotnwereuytwentmlivedopmovedtfoundkjfboughtwstartedqcworkedm

12 **Look at 11. Write the past tense form of the verbs.**

be	_was/were_	have	_____
buy	_____	live	_____
find	_____	move	_____
get	_____	start	_____
go	_____	work	_____

13 **Complete the paragraph. Use the correct form of the verbs in 12.**

My mom and dad ¹_____got_____ married when they
²_____ 24. They ³_____ with my dad's
parents because they ⁴_____ to save money
to buy their own house. They both ⁵_____ long
hours at their jobs. A few years later, they ⁶_____
a house. That ⁷_____ 15 years ago. They ⁸
_____ into the house on my mother's birthday.
I ⁹_____ born a year later!

Sue is **taller than** Yoko and Mark.

Sue is **the tallest** person in our class.

10

14 Listen and number the family members.

☐ ☐ ☐ ☐ ☐ ☐ ☐ ☐

15 Look at the picture. Complete the sentences. Use the correct form of the words.

Maria   Joan   Ben

1. **tall** Joan is _____tall_____.
   Ben is _____ than Joan.
   Ben is _____ child.

2. **young** Maria is _____.
   Maria is _____ Joan and
   Ben. Maria is _____ child.

3. **long** Maria's hair is _____ Ben's hair. Joan's hair is _____ hair of all.

16 Think of a good friend. How are you different? Write sentences. Use the words in the box.

| big | new | old | strong | tall |

1. _____
2. _____
3. _____

17 **Read. Then complete the sentences with the words in the box.**

Good and Bad Dads in the Animal Kingdom

Fathers are important in the animal kingdom. They take care of their families, and some even take care of other families, too. But some fathers are better than others.

The emu dad is a great dad. He finds grass, twigs, and leaves. Then he builds a nest for his young, all by himself. He then sits on the eggs until the baby chicks are born. During this time he doesn't eat or drink! When the chicks are born, the dad takes care of them, and teaches them how to find food.

Seahorses do something very special to protect their future offspring. The father seahorse gives birth to his young! He carries the eggs in a special pouch in his stomach for about three weeks until the baby seahorses are born. What an amazing dad!

Lions are fierce predators and can be really scary! A lion dad protects his family well, and his family can be big. There can be seven lionesses, mom lions, and twenty babies in his family. But he isn't really a great dad. He doesn't often hunt for food. The moms have to do that. The lion dad likes to sleep a lot, especially between branches in trees. He's lazy!

| offspring | predator | protect | young |

1. A _____ is an animal that eats other animals, like a lion.
2. Some mothers or fathers carry their _____ when they are very young.
3. Male seahorses give birth to their _____.
4. Dads keep their babies safe. They _____ their babies.

18 **What do you think? Circle _T_ for _True_ and _F_ for _False_.**

1. Emu chicks will die if they don't have a father.   T   F
2. Seahorses carry their young in a pouch to protect them from predators.   T   F
3. Lionesses are good hunters.   T   F

19 Read. Then answer the questions.

Special Birthdays

Families around the world celebrate birthdays in different ways.

In Nigeria, first, fifth, tenth, and fifteenth birthdays are very important. The parents have big parties for their children and more than 100 people come to the party. They eat a lot— sometimes a whole roasted cow!

Brazilian children have fun birthdays. Parents decorate the house with brightly colored banners and flowers. Brazilians also pull on the ear of the birthday boy or girl. They pull once for each year.

On the first birthday of a Hindu child in India, the parents shave the top of their child's head. When they are older they have birthday parties. They wear new clothes and give thanks to their parents by touching their parents' feet. At school the birthday child gives chocolates to classmates.

Australian children have very sweet birthdays! They eat Fairy Bread. This is a slice of bread with butter, and on the butter are a lot of small sprinkles called *hundreds and thousands*.

1. What birthdays are important in Nigeria?

   _____

2. A Brazilian boy is celebrating his eleventh birthday. How many times do his parents pull his ear?

   _____

3. What does a Hindu child do at school on his or her birthday?

   _____

4. What are *hundreds and thousands*?

   _____

20 Check the country with birthday traditions that you like the best.

☐ Nigeria   ☐ Brazil   ☐ India   ☐ Australia

An autobiography tells the important events in your life and when they happened. The events are in the order they happened. The information often includes:

- when and where you were born
- places you lived
- things you did
- your family and friends
- special memories
- your interests

21 Look at Adele's autobiography. Add events from the chart. Use the correct form of the verbs.

Dates	Events
1988	be born in London, England
1991	start singing
2006	write my first successful songs
2009	win the Grammy Award for Best New Artist
2011	have throat surgery
2009 to the present	start donating to charities

My Life

My name is Adele. My full name is Adele Laurie Blue Adkins. ¹*I was born in London, England* in 1988. I am an only child. I have no brothers or sisters, so my mother and I are very close. I ²_____ in front of my mother's friends when I was only three. I loved music and ³_____ when I was at the BRIT School for Performing Arts and Technology. I was about 18 years old. Three years later, ⁴_____. 2011 was a scary year. I ⁵_____, but I am fine now, and continue to sing and receive rewards for my work. In 2009, I ⁶_____ that help sick children and families of sick children, and to charities that help musicians in need. That is my best achievement.

22 In the Student Book, you wrote a story about your life. Write a different story on a separate piece of paper. Complete the chart and use it to help you write.

Date	Event
_____	_____
_____	_____
_____	_____
_____	_____

23 Complete the sentences. Use the correct form of the verbs in the box.

be born   buy   get married   move   start

Notes about My Family Ties

1. My brother _____ a new car last month. He is so happy.
2. I miss my grandma and grandpa. A year ago, they _____ away, and now they live in Monterey.
3. My cousin _____ art school last year. He is a really good artist.
4. I have a new baby brother. He _____ a few weeks ago. He looks like me!
5. When my parents _____, they were very young. They made a beautiful couple.

24 Complete the sentences. Use *when*, *ago*, or *later* and the correct form of the verbs.

When?	Age 16	Age 17	Age 18	Age 19	Age 21
What happened?	learn to drive	get a part-time job	start college	buy first car	graduate from college

1. Jack _____learned_____ to drive _____when_____ he _____was_____ 16.
2. He _____ a part-time job _____ he _____ 17.
3. _____ he _____ 18, he _____ college.
4. One year _____, he _____ his first car. He _____ 19.
5. He _____ from college two years _____ and now he works at a bank.

25 Complete the dialogue. Use the correct form of the words in parentheses.

A: Tell me about your family, David.

B: Well, I have three sisters, Jen, Beth, and Kim. Jen is _____ of the three. (old) Beth is _____. (young) And Kim is in the middle.

A: Really?

B: Yeah. And guess what. Beth is _____ in my family! (tall)

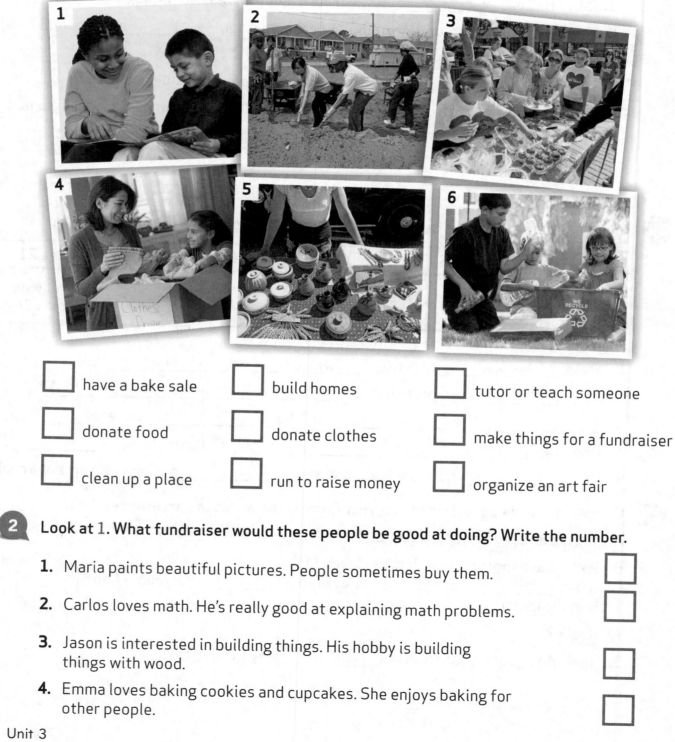

unit 3 — HELPING OTHERS

1 Which activities do you see in the pictures? Write the number.

☐ have a bake sale

☐ donate food

☐ clean up a place

☐ build homes

☐ donate clothes

☐ run to raise money

☐ tutor or teach someone

☐ make things for a fundraiser

☐ organize an art fair

2 Look at 1. What fundraiser would these people be good at doing? Write the number.

1. Maria paints beautiful pictures. People sometimes buy them. ☐

2. Carlos loves math. He's really good at explaining math problems. ☐

3. Jason is interested in building things. His hobby is building things with wood. ☐

4. Emma loves baking cookies and cupcakes. She enjoys baking for other people. ☐

3 Unscramble and write the words.

1.

rta ifar

_____

2.

ekba lesa

_____

3.

ehva a tccnoer

_____

4.

eakm a diove

_____

5.

meak soteprs

_____

6.

erwti na riatlce

_____

4 Complete the sentences with the words in 3. Then listen to check your answers.

1. Why don't we have a _____ next week at school? I can make cookies and you could make a cake.

2. Sara knows how to use the video camera. She can _____ to tell people about our event.

3. We could _____ to make money. A lot of us love to play music.

4. We could _____ and hang them up around school.

5. Let's draw and paint some things and sell them at an _____.

6. Someone could _____ for the school website.

5 The sixth-grade class wants to raise money. What could they do? How could they tell people about it? Write your suggestions.

_____

_____

6 Listen and read. Then answer the questions.

Monday, September 25 at 2:30 pm, Alex in Grade 6 wrote . . .

WE NEED MONEY!

Listen up, everyone. As you know, our school needs a lot of things. We need new computers for the computer lab, a new freezer for the cafeteria, and new chess sets for the chess club. There will soon be some fundraisers to raise money. Fundraisers are often boring, I know. But I think we could be more creative and do some fun things. I talked to some students, and here are some good ideas:

- **Karaoke competition with kids and parents.** We can sell tickets to each contestant, and parents and kids can compete against each other.

- **Temporary tattoos.** We could sell tattoos of anime characters and other fun things.

- **Students vs. teachers sports events.** I'd love to see this!! We could play basketball or ping pong. . . . Any other suggestions for sports?

- **Parents spelling bee.** Let's have our parents spell words! Could your parent win?

What do you think? Let me know. We can talk to our teachers and see if they're OK with the ideas. Maybe we could have a fundraising year that is really fun! ☺

COMMENTS

arichards
Great ideas! I'll help you! Talk to you later.

cody_thomas
The karaoke night is a really cool idea! I know my parents would be interested.

---

1. What is the blog about?

_____

2. What does the writer think about past fundraisers?

_____

3. What does the writer think about the fundraiser this year?

_____

7 What new fundraising ideas do you have? Add a comment.

_____

8  Listen. Then circle the correct answers.

Pete: That car looks great! <u>What's up?</u>

Mary: Oh, thanks. We're having this car wash to raise money for our science club. We're going to buy materials for our science projects.

Pete: <u>It's too bad</u> you don't have many people or cars.

Mary: Yes. I guess a lot of people don't realize we're doing this here.

Pete: I have an idea. Taylor and I could make signs and hold them up over there so more people will stop.

Mary: <u>What a great idea!</u> We didn't think about that!

1. What is the science club going to do with the fundraiser money?
   a. buy materials for science projects   **b.** give the money to charity

2. How many people and cars are there?
   a. a lot   **b.** not a lot

3. Does Mary like Pete's idea?
   a. yes   **b.** no

4. What are Taylor and Pete going to do?
   a. help wash cars   **b.** make signs and hold them up

9 Listen and repeat. Then circle the best meaning of each expression.

1. What's up?
   a. How are you?   **b.** What are you doing?

2. It's too bad.
   a. It's unfortunate.   **b.** It's not good.

3. What a great idea!
   a. I like your idea a lot.   **b.** I'm not sure what your idea is.

10 Complete the sentences with the expressions in 9.

1. **A:** Hey, Leslie. _____?
   B: I'm studying. What are you doing?

2. **A:** I know what we could do to make money. We could sell raffle tickets.
   B: _____. I like it a lot!

3. **A:** _____ you aren't going to be at the concert tomorrow night.
   B: I know. But I'm really sick. Have a good time without me!

Grammar

How **could** we raise money for our club?	We **could** have a car wash.
How much **could** they charge to wash one car?	They **could** charge $5 for a small car. For a bigger car, they **could** charge $8.00.

11 Complete the questions. Use *How could* or *How much could*. Then match the questions and suggestions. Write the numbers.

1. Let's have a class trip fundraiser. _____ we raise with a fundraiser?

2. _____ we charge for our winter concert tickets?

3. _____ we tell people about the fundraiser?

4. _____ we raise money to buy new band uniforms?

___ **a.** We could write articles about it in the school newspaper.

___ **b.** We could have a car wash.

___ **c.** I think we could raise a lot of money.

___ **d.** We could probably ask for $5.00 a ticket.

12 Read the sentences. Complete the sign-up sheet. Write the correct name. Then complete the sentences with *could*.

The Art Club Book Sale Sign-Up Sheet

Team 1: Collect books Monday after school	Team 2: Make posters on Tuesday after school	Team 3: Put up posters on Wednesday morning	Team 4: Sell books on Saturday	Team 5: Clean up on Saturday at 4:00
1. Jill	1. Gina	1. Carolyn	9:00–11:00: Tanya	1. Brendan
2. Samantha	2. Ben	2. _____	11:00–1:00 _Tina_	2. Jeff
3. _____	3. _____		1:00–3:00: Candy	3. _____

1. Tina is free on Saturday at 11:00. She _could sell books_____.

2. Paul is free after school on Monday. He _____.

3. Sally is free on Tuesday after school. She _____.

4. Mario is free on Saturday at 4:00. He _____.

5. Lisa is free on Wednesday morning. She _____.

13 Look at 12. How and when could you help?

_____

How **are you going to** tell people about your bake sale?

We**'re going to** make posters.

14 Complete the sentences. Use *is/am/are going to*.

Fifth Grade News

Hi Everyone!

This is a busy week! Don't forget! Our class car wash is this Saturday! We ¹_____ meet in front of the school at 7:30 in the morning. Please be on time. Bring a towel and an extra set of clothes – you ²_____ get very wet. I ³_____ bring snacks. Please bring something to drink.

Also, Carol ⁴_____ make posters this Thursday. I hope you can join her and help out. And Jeremy ⁵_____ hand out flyers to parents when they pick up their kids after school.

Now we need YOU. Join us! How ⁶_____ we _____ make this a success without you? Can you help? Let me know. And remember to tell your parents and family. I know we ⁷_____ have a great time and make lots of money!

See you there!

Mrs. Hendricks

15 Look at the students' schedule for next week. Complete the questions and answers with *am/is/are going to*.

KIDS HELPING—WEEKLY CALENDAR	Me	Peter and Hugo	Sheila
make a video of the glee club	✓		
do a long walk for charity		✓	
sell tickets for the school play			✓

1. **A:** How _____ you _____ get kids interested in joining the glee club?
   B: I _____.

2. **A:** How _____ Peter and Hugo _____ raise money for charity?
   B: They _____.

3. **A:** What _____ Sheila _____ do next week?
   B: She _____.

Creating an Effective Poster or Ad

16 Match the words and the definitions. Write the letters.

___ **1.** font
___ **2.** images
___ **3.** design
___ **4.** layout
___ **5.** effective

a. use of pictures
b. the style of the letters
c. how the information is organized
d. the way the font and images look
e. successful

17 Read. Look at the ads. Which one is more effective? Check *A* or *B*.

Advertisements tell people about a product and make people want to buy it. A successful ad has interesting design, images, and fonts. These things can add to the impact of the ad. It has to have a good layout to make the message more effective.

A

Come to the 6th grade talent show!

The glee club is going to have a talent show next Saturday.

Please come. It's going to be lots of fun!

The talent show starts at 5:30. Tickets are only $5.00.

B

Come to the 6th grade talent show!

Saturday evening.
Show starts at 5:30.

It's going to be lots of fun!

Tickets are only $5.00.

	A	B
1. The font is clear and easy to read.	☐	☐
2. The images don't tell me a lot about the talent show.	☐	☐
3. The layout isn't attractive.	☐	☐
4. The poster has a good design.	☐	☐
5. This poster makes me want to buy a ticket.	☐	☐
6. The information is clear and well organized.	☐	☐

18 What do you think? Circle *Yes* or *No*.

1. You don't need a lot of skill to make an effective advertisement.　　　**Yes**　　**No**

2. An effective advertisement can help sell a lot of a product.　　　**Yes**　　**No**

19 Read. Then circle the correct answers.

Companies That Help People

Child's Play

Being sick is no fun. Being sick in a hospital is terrible! You're alone, and you're scared. Your parents aren't there all the time. You don't have your computer, your video games, or any other games. People who worked at video game companies knew this and decided to help sick children in hospitals. They started a charity called Child's Play.

Child's Play gives video games and video game consoles to hospitals. They also give toys and books. Sick children can enjoy them all and feel a little better. Everyone can give money to Child's Play. It's a wonderful way to help children who are in hospitals.

Kiva

Kiva is a company that does what it can to help people. Kiva helps people start their own companies. For example, Josie is good at baking. She wants to start her own business and sell her delicious baked goods. But it's expensive to start your own business, and Josie doesn't have a lot of money. Kiva can help. Kiva finds people to lend Josie money to start her company. When her business becomes successful, she will give the money back to the people who helped her. People can give any amount of money to Kiva, even really small amounts. It's a great way to help others.

1. Child's Play gives video games and fun things to ___.
   a. sick children at home
   b. sick children in hospitals

2. The people who started Child's Play worked ___.
   a. in hospitals
   b. at video game companies

3. Kiva helps people who want to ___.
   a. start a company
   b. make cookies and baked goods

4. Kiva helps people find ___.
   a. people who will lend a lot of money
   b. people who will lend some money

20 What about you? Answer the question.

You have $100 for charity. Which charity do you want to help? Why?

_____

_____.

A well-written letter has clear ideas and good organization. It usually includes:

- the date
- a greeting, such as *Dear Mr. Smith:*
- the body of the letter
- a closing, such as *Sincerely,* or *Best regards,*
- your signature (your name)

The letter in this unit offers suggestions. When you write a letter that gives a suggestion, the body of the letter includes:

- your idea or suggestion
- how people can carry out the idea
- why the idea is important

21 **Write the parts of the letter.**

> body   closing   date   greeting   signature

1 _____ May 10, 2014

2 _____ Dear Mr. Green:

3 _____ I think that the school should raise money to help the Houses for All charity. This charity builds homes for homeless families. We could raise money for this charity. We could collect pennies and raise money that way, or we could have bake sales to raise money.

This project is a good one because all children deserve a good home. We can help. Please think about this idea.

4 _____ Sincerely,

5 _____ Teresa Lee

22 **Look at 21. Circle the answers in the letter.**

What is the suggestion?

How can people carry out the idea?

Why is the idea important?

23 **Write a letter to your teacher. Suggest a plan to raise money for a charity.**

24 How can these students raise money at their school fair? Write suggestions with *could*.

I'm Marie. I have a lot of books, but I don't need them.

I'm Fritz. I'm really good at painting T-shirts.

I'm Erik. I have a great video camera, and I enjoy making videos.

I'm Gaby. I really enjoy writing.

1. Marie _____.

2. Fritz _____.

3. Erik _____.

4. Gaby _____.

25 Complete the sentences. Use *is/am/are going to*.

A: How ¹_____ we ²_____ raise money for computers at school?

B: I have a plan. We ³_____ organize a contest.

A: And how ⁴_____ you ⁵_____ tell people about the contest?

B: I ⁶_____ make big posters and put them up all over school.

A: How ⁷_____ the contest ⁸_____ help raise money?

B: Maybe we could ask students to buy a ticket to be in the contest.

A: Well, I don't know … What kind of contest ⁹_____ you ¹⁰_____ have?

B: We ¹¹_____ have an online writing contest. Kids write a paragraph titled: *Why we need computers at school*. That's a great idea, right?

A: That's crazy! The school doesn't have computers! Kids can't write online.

B: Oh. Right.

Think Big

1 Look at the pictures. Write the words. Add your own words on the extra line.

My Interests

1. <u>doing martial arts</u>
2. _____
3. _____
4. _____
5. _____

Family Ties

1. _____
2. _____
3. _____
4. _____
5. _____

Helping Others

1. _____
2. _____
3. _____
4. _____
5. _____

2 Think of a famous person or a cartoon character. Complete the information about him or her.

Name _____	
Interests	He or she is interested in: _____ He or she is good at: _____ He or she likes: _____
Family Ties	Here are some family events in his or her life: _____ _____ _____
Helping Others	Here is a way he or she could help: _____ _____ Here is what he or she is going to do: _____ _____

3 Think about a song your person could like. Use **1** and **2** to help you. Choose a song and write a letter to your person about it. Explain why you chose this song.

_____

_____

_____

_____

_____

4 In Your Classroom

Work in pairs and share.

SHOPPING AROUND

1 Match the places and the pictures. Write the number.

1

2

3

4

5

6

☐ mall

☐ craft fair

☐ electronics store

☐ department store

☐ comic book store

☐ sporting goods store

2 Where do you like to shop? Check (✓) your answers.

☐ clothing store

☐ book store

☐ flower shop

☐ video game store

☐ music store

☐ jewelry store

3 Look at 1. Which places are in your neighborhood? Circle them.

4 Listen and number the pictures.

5 Where could you buy these gifts? Circle the correct answer.

1. a turquoise necklace
   - **a.** a craft fair
   - **b.** an electronics store
2. silver earrings
   - **a.** a flower shop
   - **b.** a department store
3. a beaded bracelet
   - **a.** a department store
   - **b.** a music store
4. balloons
   - **a.** a mall
   - **b.** a craft fair
5. roses
   - **a.** a bookstore
   - **b.** a flower shop
6. a handmade picture frame
   - **a.** a craft fair
   - **b.** a sporting goods store

6 Write the answers.

1. Your mom loves jewelry. What kind of jewelry could you buy her for her birthday?

   _____

2. Your mom loves flowers. What kind of flowers could you buy her for Mother's Day?

   _____

3. Your dad likes handmade things from craft fairs. What could you buy him for Father's Day?

   _____

7 Listen and read. Then check the correct person.

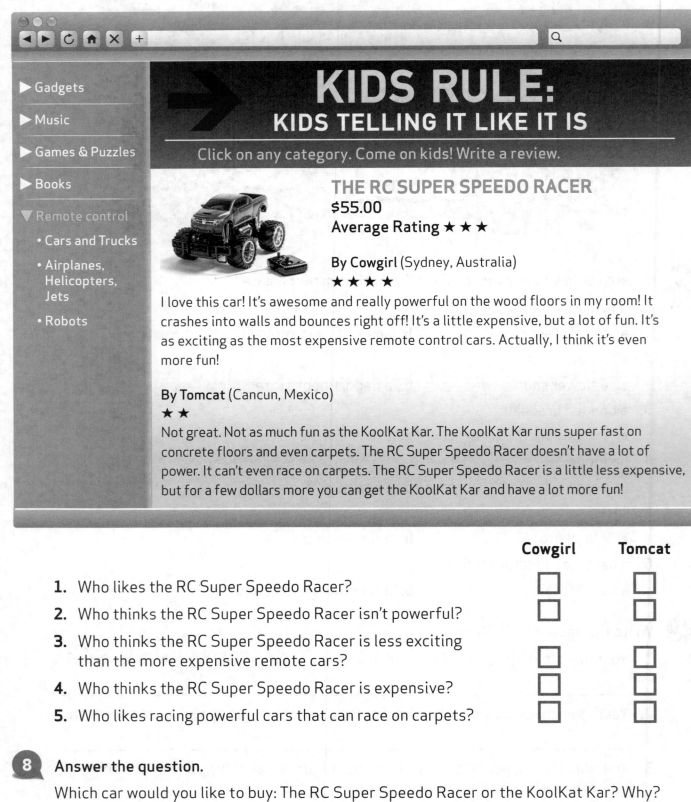

▶ Gadgets

▶ Music

▶ Games & Puzzles

▶ Books

▼ Remote control

• Cars and Trucks

• Airplanes, Helicopters, Jets

• Robots

KIDS RULE:
KIDS TELLING IT LIKE IT IS

Click on any category. Come on kids! Write a review.

THE RC SUPER SPEEDO RACER
$55.00
Average Rating ★ ★ ★

By Cowgirl (Sydney, Australia)
★ ★ ★ ★

I love this car! It's awesome and really powerful on the wood floors in my room! It crashes into walls and bounces right off! It's a little expensive, but a lot of fun. It's as exciting as the most expensive remote control cars. Actually, I think it's even more fun!

By Tomcat (Cancun, Mexico)
★ ★

Not great. Not as much fun as the KoolKat Kar. The KoolKat Kar runs super fast on concrete floors and even carpets. The RC Super Speedo Racer doesn't have a lot of power. It can't even race on carpets. The RC Super Speedo Racer is a little less expensive, but for a few dollars more you can get the KoolKat Kar and have a lot more fun!

	Cowgirl	Tomcat
1. Who likes the RC Super Speedo Racer?	☐	☐
2. Who thinks the RC Super Speedo Racer isn't powerful?	☐	☐
3. Who thinks the RC Super Speedo Racer is less exciting than the more expensive remote cars?	☐	☐
4. Who thinks the RC Super Speedo Racer is expensive?	☐	☐
5. Who likes racing powerful cars that can race on carpets?	☐	☐

8 Answer the question.

Which car would you like to buy: The RC Super Speedo Racer or the KoolKat Kar? Why?

9 Listen. Then write the answer.

Jen: How about this one? It got some really great reviews. Look.

Sam: Oh yeah? Is it as nice as yours?

Jen: Yeah ... It's a really good player, and it's the least expensive one at this store.

Eddie: Yeah but it's $85! I don't have that much money.

Jen: Yes, but look. It's on sale! Let's see, it's only $60. It has four gigabytes of memory. And it comes with a free case.

Eddie: Wow! The design is really cool, too. It's perfect!

Jen: Oh, no! There's only one problem.

Eddie: What?

Jen: It's already sold out.

Eddie: Oh, man!

1. Who knows more about mp3 players, Jen or Eddie? _____

2. Does Eddie need to buy a case for the mp3 player? _____

3. Why doesn't Eddie buy the mp3 player? _____

10 Look at 9. Read the underlined expressions. How can you say them in other words? Match and write the letter.

___ **1.** How about ...?

___ **2.** Oh, yeah?

___ **3.** Yeah.

___ **4.** Yeah but ...

___ **5.** Oh, man!

a. I'm really disappointed!

b. I know, but ...

c. What do you think of ...?

d. Really?

e. Yes.

11 Complete the sentences with the expressions in 10.

A: ¹_____ going to the craft fair now? There's a big one today.

B: ²_____ Where is it?

A: It's in the park, near school.

B: Great. Maybe I can find a birthday present for my brother.

A: ³_____.

B: Hey, did you feel that? It's raining!

A: ⁴_____. Now we can't go!

Grammar

> The blue shoes are **expensive**.
>
> The red shoes are **more expensive than** the blue shoes.
>
> The black shoes are **the most expensive** of all.
>
> The red shoes are not **as expensive as** the black shoes.

> The white shoes are **less expensive than** the blue shoes.
>
> The white shoes are **the least expensive** of all.

12 Look at the ratings. Circle the correct answers.

Movie Reviews
Category: Sci Fi

The Story	Horrible ★	Boring ★ ★	OK ★ ★ ★	Interesting ★ ★ ★ ★	Amazing ★ ★ ★ ★ ★
The Acting	Terrible ★	Disappointing ★ ★	OK ★ ★ ★	Great ★ ★ ★ ★	Extraordinary ★ ★ ★ ★ ★
Popularity	Bomb ★	Not Popular ★ ★	OK ★ ★ ★	Very Popular ★ ★ ★ ★	Extremely Popular ★ ★ ★ ★ ★

	Story	Acting	Popularity
Robots of the Universe	★ ★ ★ ★ ★	★ ★	★ ★ ★ ★
Princess of Evil	★ ★ ★ ★	★ ★ ★	★ ★ ★ ★ ★
The Pirates	★	★ ★ ★ ★ ★	★ ★ ★

1. *The Pirates* is **less / more** popular than *Princess of Evil*.

2. The story of *Princess of Evil* is **less / more** interesting than the story of *The Pirates*.

3. The acting in *Princess of Evil* is **less / more** extraordinary than the acting in *Robots of the Universe*.

4. *The Pirates* is **the most / the least** popular movie.

5. The story of *Robots of the Universe* is **the least / the most** amazing.

6. *Princess of Evil* is **the most / the least** popular movie.

13 Look at the ratings in 12. Then complete the sentences with *more/less ... than* or *the most/the least*.

1. The story of *Robots of the Universe* is _____ amazing _____ the story of the *Princess of Evil*.

2. The acting in *Robots of the Universe* is _____ extraordinary of all the movies.

3. The story in *The Pirates* is _____ boring of all.

4. The story in *The Pirates* is _____ interesting _____ the story in the other two movies.

14 Complete the sentences. Use *as . . . as* or *not as . . . as* and the words in parentheses.

1. The black jeans are _____ the blue jeans. (fashionable)
2. The black jeans are _____ the blue jeans. (cheap)
3. The blue jeans are _____ the black jeans. (baggy)
4. The black jeans are _____ the blue jeans. (popular)
5. The blue jeans are _____ the black jeans. (comfortable)

The price of those sneakers is **too** high.	The price isn't low **enough**.
Those jeans are **too** small.	The jeans aren't big **enough**.

15 Look at 14. Circle the correct answer.

1. My brother wears really baggy jeans. The blue jeans ___ for him.

   a. aren't baggy enough   **b.** are too baggy

2. I like colorful pants. Those jeans ___ for me.

   a. aren't colorful enough   **b.** are too colorful

3. I usually wear white shirts with my jeans. That shirt ___ for me.

   a. isn't bright enough   **b.** is too bright

4. We always buy jeans that are inexpensive. These jeans are perfect. The price ___.

   a. is cheap enough   **b.** is too cheap

16 Complete the puzzle with the words in the box.

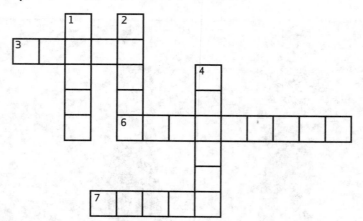

coins
livestock
metal
paper
shells
trade

ACROSS

3. Exchange one thing for another

6. Cows and goats

7. Round metal money

DOWN

1. Dollar bills and bank notes are made of this.

2. This is very shiny—silver is one type of this.

4. Some animals live in these.

17 Read. Then answer the questions. Use short answers.

The Idea for Paper Money

The story of paper money is a fascinating one. The use of bank notes started in the Tang Dynasty. The Tang Dynasty existed in China from 618–907.

Before Chinese people used paper money, they used coins. The coins were round and had a square hole in the middle. They kept their coins on a rope, so the more coins on the string they had, the heavier the rope would be. Rich people found that their ropes of coins were too heavy to carry around easily. So what did they do? They left their strings of coins with someone they trusted, and that person gave them a piece of paper with a note saying the amount of money he was keeping. When the rich man wanted his money, he took the paper to that trusted person and he got his coins back. This was a good idea, don't you think?

1. How did Chinese people keep money long ago?

_____

2. What did rich people do with their coin ropes when they were too heavy?

_____

3. What did that trusted person give the coin owner?

_____

4. How did the rich man get his coins back?

_____

18 Read. Then circle *True* or *False*.

SHOPPING Is FUN!

How to shop in Chatuchak Market, Bangkok

Chatuchak Market is a great place to bargain. Everyone bargains here. When you bargain, you try to pay a lower price for something. Here's an example. You want to buy a hat. The hat costs $20. You say to the vendor, the person who sells the hat, "I want to pay $10." The vendor says, "That's too cheap. How about $15?" You say, "No way! That's still too expensive. How about $12?" The vendor says, "OK, $12." Because you bargained, you just paid $8 less for the hat!

Bargaining is a good skill to have when you shop in some places. You can buy things for less money, and this means you can buy more things.

Mandarake in Akihabara, Tokyo

The most popular place in Akihabara could be Mandarake. This is the largest manga and anime store in the world. The store includes all eight floors in a building. It's full of DVDs of anime movies, comic books, and action figures of your favorite characters. The customers who shop at Akihabara are very interesting, too. Some of them dress up to look like the characters in animation movies, like Sailor Moon, Pokemon, and Super Mario. These people wear costumes and makeup and really enjoy acting like their favorite characters.

1. You can bargain at Chatuchak Market.	**True**	**False**
2. When you bargain, you want to pay more for something.	**True**	**False**
3. Mandarake is the largest manga and anime store in the world.	**True**	**False**
4. Some customers in Mandarake dress up like sports heroes.	**True**	**False**

19 Circle and complete the sentences.

1. I **want to / don't want to** go to Chatuchak Market because _____

_____

2. I **want to / don't want to** go to Akihabara because _____

_____

A good product review tells what is good and bad about a product and gives a recommendation. A recommendation tells the readers if they should buy the product.

Here are ways to say if a product is good or bad:

Good

It's the best.
They're worth the money.
It's great.

Bad

It's terrible.
They're not worth the money.
It isn't great.

Here are ways to give a recommendation:

I definitely recommend this product.
This product isn't great, but [tell why some people might like it].
I don't recommend this product because . . .

Remember to explain your ideas.

20 Read the product review. Answer the questions. Write the sentence numbers.

¹I bought my Wrap-Arounds at Cheap Charlie. ²They aren't great headphones, but they're good for people who don't have a lot of money. ³You can buy more expensive headphones and get more amazing sound, but why? ⁴I think they're worth the money, especially if you don't need to hear an extraordinary sound. ⁵I recommend Wrap-Arounds because they have good sound for little money.

Which sentences explain . . .

1. who would like the headphones? ☐

2. why the headphones are worth the money? ☐

3. if you should buy the headphones? ☐

21 Choose a gadget you have or want. Write a review.

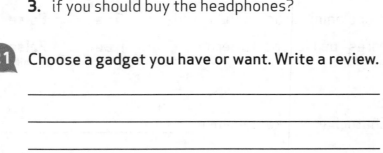

_____

_____

_____

_____

_____

TIPS

To write a good review you need to decide these things:

1. Do you like the product or not? Why or why not?

2. What is good or bad about it?

3. Is it worth the money?

4. Will you recommend it or not?

22 Write the words in the correct column.

> bracelet   clothing store   craft fair   digital camera   earrings
> flower shop   headphones   mp3 player   necklace

Jewelry	Gadgets	Places
bracelet		

23 Look at the ratings. Complete the sentences. Write *more/less popular...than*, and *the most/the least popular*.

★★★★★   ★★★   ★★★★

1. The gold bracelet is _____ the beaded bracelet.
2. The beaded bracelet is _____ the silver bracelet.
3. The gold bracelet is _____ of them all.
4. The beaded bracelet is _____ of them all.

24 Write the sentences. Use *too* or *not enough* and the words in parentheses.

1. These shoes look like boats on my feet. They're
   _____. (big)

2. Wow! This digital camera costs a lot of money. It's
   _____. (expensive)

3. I can't hear the video. It's _____. (loud)

4. These headphones always break. They're _____ (strong).

VACATION TIME

1 Which vacations do you see in the pictures? Write the numbers.

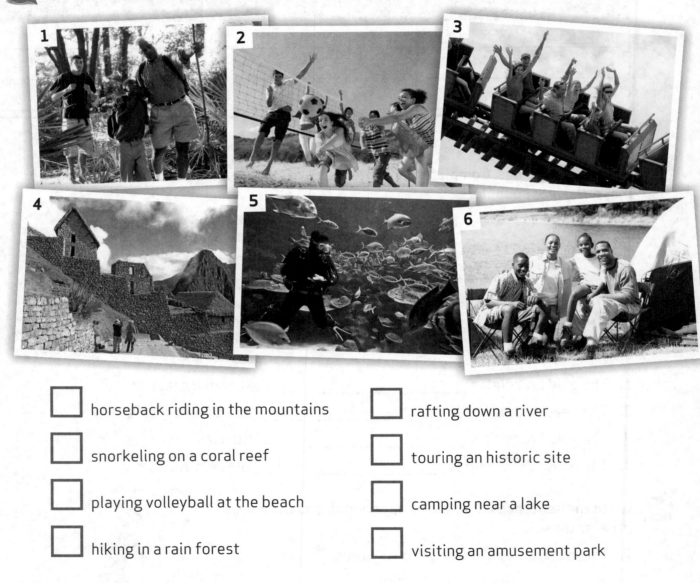

☐ horseback riding in the mountains

☐ snorkeling on a coral reef

☐ playing volleyball at the beach

☐ hiking in a rain forest

☐ rafting down a river

☐ touring an historic site

☐ camping near a lake

☐ visiting an amusement park

2 Look at 1. Which vacation would you like the best? Which vacation would you like the least? Rank the vacations and write their numbers in the chart.

The least 👍	👍👍	👍👍👍	👍👍👍👍	The most 👍👍👍👍👍

3 Write the words in the correct column.

> bug repellent   a helmet   a life vest   a map   sunglasses
> sunscreen   a warm jacket   a water bottle   a windbreaker

useful clothing	
useful for eyes	
useful for skin	
useful for safety/health	

4 Look at 3. Complete the sentences.

1. I'm wearing _____ because there are a lot of bugs in the woods.

2. Take _____. You'll get thirsty on the hike.

3. When you go horseback riding, wear _____. You could fall.

4. I'm glad we took _____ on our bike trip. We almost got lost.

5. It was very cold in the mountains, so I wore _____.

6. The captain of the boat gave me _____ because the water was rough and dangerous.

7. I didn't wear enough _____ at the beach, and now I have a sunburn.

8. When you walk on the beach in winter, it can be windy and chilly. Be sure to wear _____.

5 Look at 3. Answer the question. Write the words.

> I'm going to go biking on a forest path on a very sunny day.
> It is sometimes windy in the afternoons.
> What should I take to be comfortable and safe?

_____, _____, _____,

_____, _____

_____, and _____

6 Listen and read. Then answer the questions.

A Family's Kayaking Trip

Joey felt awful when he woke up. His head hurt. His stomach hurt. His ears hurt. He was sad because his family was going kayaking soon. His mom looked at him and said, "Sorry, Joey, you're too sick to go with us. You have to stay home with Grandma." Joey was mad! It wasn't fair!

His family said goodbye and left. Joey was staring at the TV when his grandma came in. She said, "Don't worry, Joey. You'll go kayaking another day."

Joey stared at the ceiling. He was thinking about his family. They were probably having a wonderful time. He closed his eyes and pictured them. They were in their kayaks on the river, laughing and having fun. There were deer and bears on the river banks and birds everywhere.

He was sleeping when his family returned. He woke up as they entered his room. They looked miserable. His mom said, "We had the worst time. We all got mosquito bites. I fell and hurt my arm on the way to the river. Your sister fell into the river when she got out of her kayak. Your dad hit his head on a tree branch hanging over the river. You're very lucky that you stayed home."

1. What did Joey's family do?

   _____

2. Why didn't Joey go with his family?

   _____

3. How did Joey imagine his family's day?

   _____

4. Why was Joey surprised when he saw his family?

   _____

7 Answer the questions. Explain your answers.

1. Do you think Joey still wants to go kayaking?

   _____

2. Do you think his family wants to go kayaking again?

   _____

3. Do you want to go kayaking?

   _____

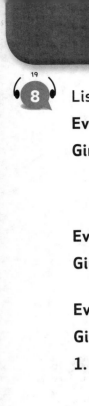

8 Listen. Then circle the correct answers.

Eve: So how did your vacation go?

Gina: It was terrible. On the second day, we went shopping in a small town. I was pretty excited at first. One shop had great souvenirs. You know, t-shirts and magnets, stuff like that.

Eve: I bet you got something wonderful.

Gina: Well, I had my eye on a really cute pair of earrings. But while I was shopping, I lost my wallet. By the time I found it, all the shops were closed!

Eve: Aw, that's too bad. But I guess you saved a lot of money that way!

Gina: Ha! Ha! Very funny!

1. Did Gina have a good time?

    a. Yes, she did.

    b. No, she didn't.

2. Did Gina really think Eve was funny?

    a. Yes, she did.

    b. No, she didn't.

9 Look at 8. Read the underlined expressions. Think about the meaning. Then circle the correct answers.

1. Eve asks, "How did it go?" What does she want to know?

    a. How did Gina travel to the shops?

    b. What happened when Gina went shopping?

2. What other "stuff like that" can you buy at a souvenir store?

    a. postcards, tourist books, and maps

    b. stoves, refrigerators, and desks

3. What does Eve mean when she says, "I bet"?

    a. I guess.

    b. I know.

4. Gina "had her eye on" earrings. What did she want to do?

    a. She wanted to buy them.

    b. She looked at them closely.

5. When Eve says, "too bad," what does she mean?

    a. I'm sorry you didn't feel well.

    b. I'm sorry the stores were closed.

10 Complete the sentences with the expressions in 8.

A: Last week I went to a great Mexican market. I ¹_____ some cool scarves there. ²_____ you'd like them. They were in your favorite colors.

B: What else did they have there?

A: Local food and candy, traditional pottery . . . ³_____. It was all amazing!

Grammar

What **was** he **doing** when he got hurt?	He **was riding** a horse when he got hurt.
What happened while they **were hiking**?	They got lost while they **were hiking**.

11 Find and circle the 8 verbs in the iguana's tail. Use the verbs to answer the question.

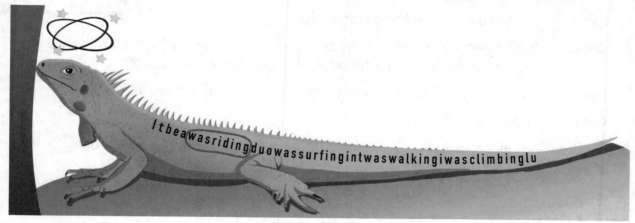

Itbeawasridingduowassurfingintwaswalkingiwasclimbinglu

What was the iguana doing when it got hurt?

1. It _____ *was riding* _____.

2. _____.

3. _____.

4. _____.

12 Match the two parts of the sentences. Write the letters.

___ **1.** While Jack was hiking in the snowy mountains . . .

___ **2.** Sue and Ben sang songs . . .

___ **3.** Steve was riding his bicycle . . .

___ **4.** When Jim and his mom were driving to the airport, . . .

a. he got lost and very cold.

b. when he rode into a tree.

c. they realized they didn't have the plane tickets!

d. while they were kayaking down the river.

13 Look at 12. Answer the questions.

1. What was Jack doing when he got lost in the mountains? _____

_____

2. What happened while Sue and Ben were singing? _____

_____

3. What was Steve doing when he hit a tree? _____

_____

Was he riding his bike when it started to rain?	Yes, he was. / No, he wasn't.
Were you swimming when you got a sunburn?	Yes, I was. / No, I wasn't.

14 Complete the questions with the correct form of *wear*. Then write the answers.

1. __Was he wearing__ sunglasses when you saw him on the beach?

   __Yes, he was.__

2. _____ life vests when they got splashed by a wave?

   _____.

3. _____ a jacket when she climbed up Big Mountain?

   _____.

4. _____ a hat when you saw her?

   _____.

5. _____ a helmet when he fell off his bike?

   _____.

6. _____ sunscreen when you saw her at the beach?

   _____.

15 Read. Then circle the correct answer.

Jim's Problem

Jim was lying on the beach when he realized he had a sunburn. He also was hungry and thirsty. So he went to Beach Shack. He wanted to buy some things. He picked out three bags of chips, a bottle of water, and some sunscreen. But while Jim was totaling the cost, he realized he had a problem. He didn't have enough money! He could solve his problem, but he had to make some choices. He had to return two bags of chips.

Oh, no! I only have $9.33

BEACH SHACK

CHIPS $1.09
WATER $1.25
SUNSCREEN $6.99

1. How much more money did Jim need?
   a. $11.51   **b.** $2.18

2. How did Jim solve his problem?
   a. He bought one bag of chips.   **b.** He bought a bottle of water.

3. How many items did Jim buy?
   a. He bought five items.   **b.** He bought three items.

4. What math did Jim use to find the totals?
   a. addition only   **b.** addition and multiplication

16 What about you? How would you solve the problem?

_____

_____

_____

_____

_____

_____

_____

_____

17 Read. Then circle *True or False*.

A Stay-cation in France

Vacations are wonderful times to be with family and explore new places and cultures. Sometimes families like to stay home. They don't like to travel, but they like to explore new places and cultures. How can they do both? These families take a "stay-cation."

Here is how a stay-cation works. Your family decides on a culture and country that they want to know more about. They do research and find out about that culture's music, crafts, food, art, and other things. Then they try to create the culture in their home during the vacation.

For example, say that your family wants to learn more about French culture. Your family would do research and find out the following things:

- popular French food
- popular French music
- popular French stories
- French art
- French holidays and other events
- the French language

During the stay-cation, your family would plan activities to do together to learn about French culture. You might eat at French restaurants, study French artists at a museum, and see French movies.

Stay-cations are great ways to enjoy your family, stay home, and learn about the world, too!

On a stay-cation, families

1. stay at homes around the world.	True	False
2. learn about interesting places and cultures from home.	True	False
3. are not interested in other places and cultures.	True	False
4. learn together.	True	False

18 Imagine you will take a stay-cation. Answer the questions.

1. What culture would you like to learn about?

_____

2. What are two things you would like to learn about that culture?

_____

_____

Writing postcards is a great way to share your vacation with friends and families. Choose a postcard with a picture of a place you visited or plan on visiting. On the other side there is a space for the address of the person you are writing to and a space for a short note about the picture or your trip. A postcard note includes, in this order:

- the **date** (*July 5*)
- a **greeting** (*Hi* or *Dear …*)
- a **body** with information about the place or your plans. (*I'm having a great time! We went to the beach yesterday.*)
- a **closing** (*See you soon!* or *I miss you!*)

Don't forget to sign your name. You want your friends and family to know the postcard comes from you! And on the right side of the note part of the card, don't forget to put the full address of the person you are writing to (name, street address, city, state, country). Remember to leave space for this address.

19 **Write the parts of the postcard.**

1 _____ See you soon!

2 _____ Dear Aunt Edna,

3 _____ August 22

4 _____ I'm so happy. I'm having an amazing time with my family in South Africa. The weather is warm. The animals in the safari park were cool. Tomorrow we are going to Cape Town. See you soon.

20 **Imagine you are visiting a place you know well. Answer these questions.**

What is the name of the place? _____

What are you doing there? _____

What exciting things have you seen? _____

Are you enjoying yourself? Why or why not? _____

What is your teacher's address at school? _____

21 **Use your answers in 20. Write a postcard to your teacher about that place.**

22 Find and circle the words. Then write the words in the correct column.

> biking   campsite   helmet   rafting   skiing   tent

c	s	d	x	d	g	d	v	m	c
r	a	f	t	i	n	g	r	e	k
n	g	m	t	f	a	s	g	k	u
g	o	t	p	l	k	i	n	g	n
e	b	l	o	s	k	i	i	n	g
u	i	g	t	u	i	g	l	d	i
l	k	o	i	f	g	t	e	n	t
t	i	i	h	e	l	m	e	t	g
o	n	w	r	i	t	i	n	g	a
n	g	a	e	n	t	t	g	i	t
r	c	f	o	i	a	s	f	n	o

Vacation activities

_____

_____

_____

Vacation things

_campsite_____

_____

_____

23 Complete the sentences. Use the correct form of the words in the box.

> driving   looking   putting on   reading

1. We _____ to the amusement park when it started to rain.

2. My dad _____ at a map when he saw the bear right in front of him!

3. My mom got a sunburn while she _____ her book on the beach.

4. I _____ sunscreen when I got stung by a bee.

24 Read. Then answer the questions.

> Yesterday morning, Tim and Jill were swimming in the lake. Yesterday afternoon, Jill went hiking while Tim was at a picnic.

1. Was Tim hiking yesterday morning?

   _____

2. Was Jill hiking yesterday afternoon?

   _____

3. Were Tim and Jill swimming in the lake yesterday?

   _____

THE FUTURE

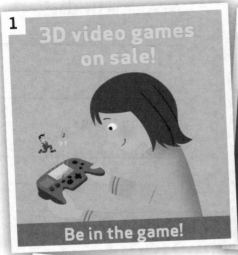

1 3D video games on sale!

Be in the game!

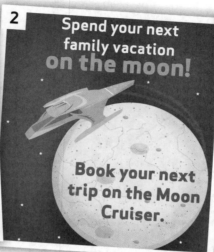

2 Spend your next family vacation on the moon!

Book your next trip on the Moon Cruiser.

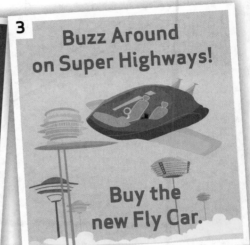

3 Buzz Around on Super Highways!

Buy the new Fly Car.

4 Chameleon Clothes!

Clothes that Change Colors!

Buy now and save!

5 Live in a Smartie House with Robot Help!

Never clean up again!

1 Which of these inventions do you think will be common in stores by 2020? Check (✓) your answer.

☐ 3D video games
☐ Moon Cruiser
☐ Fly Car
☐ Chameleon Clothes
☐ Robot Help

2 Look at 1. Which inventions would you like to buy? Circle the numbers.

1   2   3   4   5

3 What can you do with these electronic devices? Check (✓) your answer.

	You can...			
	smartphone	mp3 player	tablet	laptop computer
1. Make phone calls	✓			
2. Write essays and do homework				
3. Listen to music				
4. Watch movies and play games				
5. Text people				

4 Unscramble the words. Use the words in 3.

1. She listens to music on her _____.   3pm lpyrae
2. They read stories on their _____.   ptmsrahneo
3. He watches movies on his _____.   taetbl
4. He does his homework on his _____.   ptlopa mopetcur

5 Answer the questions.

1. Do you use electronic devices to do homework? What devices do you use?

   _____

2. Do you use electronic devices to play games? Which devices do you use?

   _____

3. Do you like electronic devices? Which device is your favorite?

   _____

6 Listen and read. Then answer the questions.

Jenny's Bad Morning

Jenny, a fifth grader, was sleeping when her bed started shaking. While the bed was shaking, a strange voice said, "Jenny, wake up! Time to go to school!" "You'll wake everybody up! Stop shaking and talking!" Jenny said. "Sorry," said the bed.

"I'm hungry," said Jenny. "Good morning, Jenny," a robot chair said. She sat on the robot and patted it. The robot carried her to the kitchen. "What would you like for breakfast, Jenny?" asked the refrigerator.

Jenny said, "Crunchy Crisp Cereal and toast, please." Five seconds later, the refrigerator opened up and put a bowl of cold cereal in front of her, and the toaster added hot toast with butter.

After breakfast, Jenny sat on the robot chair again, and it took her to her room. Jenny got dressed. "These clothes are too tight," said Jenny. The robot said, "Clothes, be bigger." The clothes got a little bigger. "Perfect!" said Jenny.

It was time for school. Jenny's mom said, "Hurry up, Jenny, get in the Fly Car." "Fly Car? No one rides in Fly Cars anymore," thought Jenny. Jenny wanted to use a Flying Suit to fly her to school. Her mom shook her head. "Sorry, you can't use a Flying Suit until you turn twelve." Jenny got in the Fly Car. She wasn't happy. She hated being eleven! She thought, "I want to be twelve! It will be so much more fun."

1. How does Jenny wake up?

_____

2. Who makes Jenny's breakfast?

_____

3. How does Jenny get to school?

_____

4. Does Jenny like the Fly Car? Why or why not?

_____

7 Answer the question.

Would you like Jenny's life? Why or why not?

_____

_____

8 Listen. Then write the answer.

Mom: Jason, <u>come on</u>. It's time to get ready for school.

Jason: Oh, Mom. Do I have to?

Mom: Yes! Get your books ready while I <u>boot up</u> your teacher on your tablet.

Jason: OK. <u>Gosh!</u> I was watching a really cool show.

Mom: At least you don't have to take the bus for an hour to school anymore. Your teacher is right here for you all the time. You just need to <u>switch</u> him <u>on</u>!

Jason: Yeah. But this robot teacher is stricter than the human ones were!

Mom: That's good. Maybe you'll learn more!

1. Where is Jason?

   _____

2. Where does Jason go to school?

   _____

3. How does Jason start classes with his teacher?

   _____

4. Why does Jason prefer human teachers to robot teachers?

   _____

9 Look at **8**. Read the underlined expressions. How can you say them in other words? Match and write the letter.

___ **1.** come on   **a.** I'm surprised. I'm disappointed.

___ **2.** boot up   **b.** Hurry! Let's go.

___ **3.** Gosh!   **c.** start the computer

___ **4.** switch on   **d.** turn on

10 Complete the sentences with the expressions in **9**.

Mom: ¹_____, Emma. It's 3 o'clock. You'll be late for the soccer game.

Emma: Oh, Mom!

Mom: ²_____! It's raining!

Emma: That's OK. I'll ³_____ my laptop and play online.

Mom: Good idea. I'll ⁴_____ the lights for you. It's getting dark.

| Do you think we **will have** cars 100 years from now? | Yes, we **will**. But cars **won't have** drivers! They'll use computers. |
| | No, we **won't**. We'll have spaceships. |

11 Look at the pictures. Complete the sentences. Use *will* or *won't*. Then listen to check your answers.

1. In 2020, smartphones _____ look the same as they do today.

2. In the future, you _____ wear your phone on your wrist.

3. In a few years from now, you _____ carry your computer in your pocket.

4. In the future, people _____ carry large tablets anymore.

5. In the future, people probably _____ listen to music on an mp3 player.

6. With one Patchster patch near each ear, you and your friends _____ be able to listen to music at the same time.

12 Complete the questions and answers. Use *will* and *won't*.

1. Do you think computers _____ roll up in the future?

   _____

2. Do you think smartphones _____ be as smart as you?

   _____

Who **will use** video messaging in the future?	**Anyone** with a computer and Internet access will use video messaging.
Who **will send** letters to communicate with friends in the future?	**No one/Nobody** will send letters to communicate with friends.
	Everyone/Everybody will use email.
	Well, **someone** might write a letter!

13 Read the class survey. Then circle the correct words.

Mrs. Brown's Class Survey—Which activities will we do in 2020?	
Will we . . .	Percentage of people who say "yes"
1. drive solar-powered cars?	100%
2. read paper books?	10%
3. go to Mars on spaceships for a vacation?	0%
4. use non-digital cameras?	0%
5. send paper birthday cards?	20%

Mrs. Brown's class survey predicts that the following statements will come true. Complete the sentences. Circle the correct word. Use the class survey.

1. ___ will drive solar-powered cars.

   a. Everybody **b.** Someone

2. ___ will read paper books.

   a. No one **b.** Someone

3. ___ will go to Mars on spaceships for a vacation.

   a. Someone **b.** Nobody

4. ___ will use non-digital cameras. They'll take pictures with digital cameras and smartphones.

   a. No one **b.** Someone

5. ___ who likes to write will send paper birthday cards. Everyone else will send email cards.

   a. Nobody **b.** Anyone

14 Circle the sentences in 13 that you agree with. Write one sentence that you don't agree with. Explain why.

I don't think that _____ because _____.

Read. Then complete the chart.

TOMORROW'S ROBOTS

We all know that robots will be part of our future. In fact, in some factories robots already make a lot of things. We aren't sure what these robotic creatures of the future will do, but many will surely be socially assistive robots. They will help us do things that are too dangerous for people to do. That's cool, right?

Firefighter Robot
One day there will be robots that fight fires. Human firefighters will control the robots and guide them into burning buildings. These robots will be able to walk, climb up ladders, and see through smoke. They might make some human gestures, too. They will help firefighters find people in the buildings.

Running Robot
There might also be some robots that look like animals. They'll probably have four legs and be able to run very fast. They'll have bigger back legs than front legs so that they can jump too. These robots will probably help police catch bad guys. They'll catch the bad guys because they'll be able to run faster than humans.

Jumping Robot
This robot won't look like an animal or a person, but it will do amazing things. It will have wheels that move it from place to place. What's amazing about this robot is that it will be able to jump very high. In fact it might be able to jump over walls or jump onto rooftops. It will help police see if there are dangerous things or people there.

Robot	What It Can Do	Who and How It Will Help
1. Firefighter Robot		
2. Running Robot		
3. Jumping Robot		

16 **Answer the questions.**

1. Which robot do you like best? _____

2. Which robot do you think helps people the most? _____

17 Read. Then circle *True* or *False*.

SAVING LANGUAGES: NOW AND LONG AGO

Khang: Vietnam
The Khang language and culture is one of the most endangered languages in Vietnam. There are only 4,000 speakers, and they don't have a written language. UNESCO (United Nations Educational, Scientific and Cultural Organization) decided to help keep the Khang language and culture from disappearing. UNESCO workers wrote down Khang traditions, developed an alphabet, prepared materials for teaching the language in classes, and trained local speakers to teach those classes.

1. The Khang language always had an alphabet.   **True**   **False**
2. The Khang people are studying their language in classes today.   **True**   **False**
3. Teaching the Khang language to young people will make the language endangered.   **True**   **False**

18 Answer the questions.

1. What languages do you want to speak well? _____
   _____
   _____

2. What ways can people save endangered languages? _____
   _____
   _____

3. Would you like to learn Khang? Why or why not? _____
   _____
   _____

4. Imagine you are the last speaker of a language. What do you want people to know about your language?
   _____
   _____

A diary is a special notebook. People often write about their day in this notebook. They write about the things that happened, and they write about their feelings or thoughts during the day. Many people like writing in their diary every day. Some people share their diary entries. Some people write only for themselves. A diary entry is similar to a letter. It includes:

- a greeting (*Dear Diary, Hello*)
- an opening sentence. It usually tells the topic of your entry. (*I'm very happy today.*)
- the body. It includes a lot of information about the topic.
- a closing. (*Good night, Love, Bye*)
- your name

19 Label the parts of the diary entry.

1 _____ Dear Diary,

2 _____ We studied about the future today in school.

3 _____ I started thinking about my life in the future. In five

years, everyone in my class will be in high school. I

hope I'll have a boyfriend and that he's cute! I won't be

able to drive, but I hope that Mom and Dad will let me

stay out late. I'm tired now, so I'll say goodbye.

4 _____ Good night,

5 _____ Pat

20 Look at 19. Circle the correct answer.

1. What comes after the greeting?   **a.** a period (.)   **b.** a comma (,)   **c.** nothing
2. What comes after the closing?   **a.** a period (.)   **b.** a comma (,)   **c.** nothing
3. What comes after the writer's name?   **a.** a period (.)   **b.** a comma (,)   **c.** nothing

21 Imagine your life in six years' time. Write a diary entry about you and your life. Use 19 and 20 to help you.

22 Look at the chart. Then complete the sentences. Use *will* or *won't*.

My Predictions about the Year 2020	I don't think we will have these things! Bye-bye!	I think these things will definitely be here!
1. text friends	with cell phones	with smartphones
2. write papers	on laptops—parents might use them	on tablets
3. listen to music	on mp3 players	on Patchster-like devices
4. buy items	mostly online using computers	mostly online using electronic gadgets

1. I think people _____ with cell phones. We _____ smartphones.

2. We _____ on tablets in 2020. We _____ on laptops.

3. In the future, we _____ on mp3 players. We _____ on Patchster.

4. I think we _____ mostly online using our electronic gadgets. We _____ online using computers.

23 Look at 22. Complete the sentences. Use *Everybody* or *Nobody*.

1. _____ will use cell phones.

2. _____ will write papers on laptops.

3. _____ will listen to Patchster.

4. _____ listen to music on mp3 players.

24 Answer the questions. Use your own ideas.

1. Do you think people will carry umbrellas in the future? Why or why not?

_____

2. Do you think we'll read only electronic books in the year 2025 instead of paper books? Why or why not?

_____

Think Big

1 Look at the pictures. What are they? Write the words.

Shopping Around

1. a bracelet
2. _____
3. _____
4. _____

Vacation Time

1. _____ 3. _____
2. _____ 4. _____

The Future

1. _____
2. _____
3. _____
4. _____

2 Find or think of a song that talks about shopping, a vacation, or the future. Complete the chart.

Song title	
Singer	
Is the song in English? What language is the song?	
What is it about?	
Why do you like listening to this song?	
Is it the most popular song now?	
What were you doing when you first heard it?	
Do you think it will be popular next year?	

3 Write a review of the song for your school newspaper. Use the information in 1 and 2 to help you.

4 In Your Classroom

Work in pairs and share.

WHAT'S THAT?

1 Look at the pictures. Match these gadgets to their uses. Write the letters.

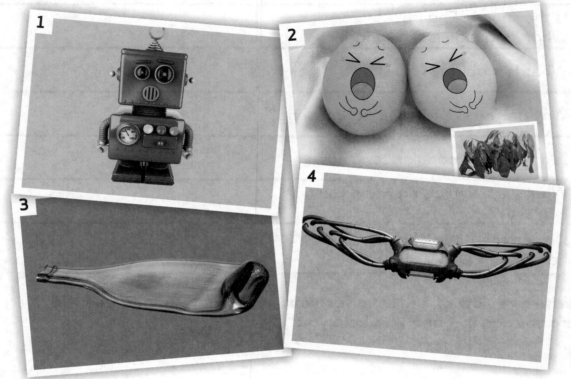

___ **Picture 1.** This is used for ...

___ **Picture 2.** This is used for ...

___ **Picture 3.** This is used for ...

___ **Picture 4.** This is used for ...

a. listening to music. You wear this headband. It plays music that only YOU can hear. It's a Music Headband.

b. doing research. You ask it questions and it tells you the answers. It helps you find information. It's Robo-pedia.

c. watering plants. The egg cries when the plant is dry. It's an Egg Plant.

d. drinking. You can fill it up with soda and drink it. When you are finished, you can wrap it up and put it away. It's a Roll-up Bottle.

2 Which gadgets do you like? Rate them. 1 = It's awesome! 2 = It's cool. 3 = It's OK. 4 = It's boring/not interesting.

a. Robo-pedia ___

b. Egg Plant ___

c. Roll-up Bottle ___

d. Music Headband ___

3 Match the old things to the modern things. Write the number.

1.   2.   3.   4.

a.   b.   c.   d.

_____   _____   _____   _____

4 Look at the pictures. Look at 3. Write the names. Use the words in the box. Listen and circle the correct answer.

> cell phone   handheld game device   instant camera   transistor radio

1. A _____ is used to
   a. play video games at home.   **b.** play games outside.

2. A _____ is used mostly to
   a. talk to people.   **b.** record messages.

3. An _____ is used mostly to
   a. take pictures.   **b.** make movies.

4. A _____ is used to
   a. record music and the news.   **b.** listen to music and the news.

5 What do you think about the future of these items ? Explain your answers.

1. People use maps to find the location of places now. Will maps be used in the future?

   _____

2. Will telephone books be used to find people's addresses and telephone numbers?

   _____

3. People use watches to tell time now. Will they be used in the future?

   _____

6 Listen and read. Then answer the questions.

CAST

Ann, Jim (classmates) | **Ms. Alba (teacher)**

SETTING A fifth-grade classroom in the year 2015.
*[The class finds a time capsule that the school made in 1990.
They open it and are looking at the things inside it.]*

Ann: *[picking up a thin square object]* Look at this. What is it?

Jim: *[takes it from her and looks at it carefully]* I'm not sure. It's plastic and it has a hole in the middle.

Ann: Hmm . . . I think it was used for watching movies on a computer.

Jim: I don't think so. I don't think people could watch movies on computers in 1990.

Ann: You're right.

Jim: *[picking up a thick rectangular object]* And what's this? It's some kind of small machine.

Ann: *[presses one of the buttons and it starts working]* Hey, it's an old music player. *[Ann puts the headphones to her ears]*

Jim: *[putting his hands over his ears]* Oh, no! I don't want to listen to old music!

Ann: *[laughing]* Someone's going to say the same thing about our music in the future. I kind of like this music. I'm going to take it to my grandfather. He might remember this kind of music.

[A teacher enters]

Jim: *[holding up the thin square object]* Hi, Ms. Alba. What's this?

Ms. Alba: Oh, that's a floppy disk. People used them to keep information from a computer on it. That way they had the information even if their computer got lost.

Jim: I see.

Ann: It's fun looking at these old things.

1. What did Ann pick up?

   _____

2. What did she think it was used for?

   _____

3. Did Jim like the music?

   _____

4. What did people use the square object for?

   _____

7 Answer the questions.

How old does something have to be for you to think it is "old"? Why?

_____

8 Listen and read. Circle *True* or *False*.

Iris: What's in the box?

Laura: It's not a box. See? It doesn't open. My grandfather brought it back from China when he went there many years ago.

Iris: Let's see. It's hard and looks like it would break if you dropped it.

Laura: Well, it would! It's made of ceramic, like the plates and dishes we use for eating.

Iris: OK. But what is it? What is it used for?

Laura: You won't believe it, but it's a pillow!

Iris: A pillow? But it's so hard!

Laura: A long time ago, women in Asia had very beautiful hairstyles that took a lot of work to create. They didn't want to ruin them by sleeping on a soft pillow. So they just rested their necks on a ceramic pillow like this one. So it was used for keeping their hair in place.

Iris: Wow! That doesn't sound very comfortable.

1. The item is a pillow made of plastic.	**True**	**False**
2. It was used when women were sleeping.	**True**	**False**
3. Iris thinks it is a good pillow.	**True**	**False**

9 Look at 8. Read the underlined expressions. How can you say them in other words? Match and write the letter.

___ **1.** See?

___ **2.** You won't believe it.

___ **3.** Let's see.

___ **4.** keep (their hair) in place

a. It's surprising.

b. Look closely.

c. keep (their hair) from getting messy

d. Let me think.

10 Complete the dialogue. Use the expressions in 9.

A: What were those bones used for?

B: ¹_____. Now I remember.
²_____, but those bones were used for a children's game called knucklebones!

A: How did women in ancient Greece
³_____ their clothes_____?

B: Well, look at this picture. ⁴_____? They wrapped their cloth around themselves and used pins or belts.

Grammar

| What's it **used** for? | It's **used** for listening to music. |
| | It's **used** to listen to music. |

11 **Match and write the letter.**

___ **1.** A hands-free ear piece is used for

___ **2.** A cell phone is used to

___ **3.** A video game system is used to

___ **4.** A handheld game device is used for

a. play video games.

b. making phone calls.

c. playing video games.

d. make phone calls.

12 **Look and read. Answer the questions with *used for* or *used to*.**

> keeping shoes on   tell time   playing video games   listen to music

1.

A: What are they used for?

B: _They're used to listen to music._

2.

A: What are they used for?

B: _____

3.

A: What's it used for?

B: _____

4.

A: What's it used for?

B: _____

| What is it? | I'm not sure. It **may** be a small plate. |
| | It **might** be a candy dish. |

13 What do you think these old things are? Use the words from the box and *may* or *might* to write sentences.

| broom | foot warmer | iron | tooth puller |

1.

<u>It may be a foot warmer.</u>

2.

_____

3.

_____

4.

_____

14 Look at the items in 13. What do you think they were used for? Write sentences with *used to*.

1. _____

2. _____

3. _____

4. _____

15 Complete the chart with inventions. Use the words in the box.

> candle   cash register   combustion engine   plumbing

How the inventions help people	Invention
1. We can easily take a shower and wash dishes and clothes.	
2. We can travel by vehicles on land, sea, and air.	
3. We can see at night when the lights go out.	
4. Stores can keep their money safely.	

16 Read. Then answer the questions.

Everyday Inventions

Who do you think of when you hear the word *inventor*? Do you think of Thomas Edison, the inventor of the light bulb, or Karl Benz, the inventor of the gas-powered car?

Not all inventors are world-famous. In fact, we don't know the names of a lot of inventors who invented some of the small useful things we use every day. For example, everyone knows about the bendable straw. But does anyone know the name Joseph Friedman? In 1937 he invented the bendable straw.

Joseph's brother owned a soda store. One day Joseph was watching his small daughter drink a milkshake from a long straw. The straw was long and she couldn't reach the end of it easily with her mouth. You may not think this is a problem, but Joseph did! He said, "Let's see. I'll put a screw into the straw, and wrap floss around it on the outside of the straw." He tried it and then he took the screw out. The straw could bend, and the bendable straw was born.

screw

floss

bendable straw

1. Who was with Joseph Friedman at his brother's store? _____

2. What problem was she having? _____

3. What did Joseph Friedman put inside and outside the straw? _____

4. What was the result? _____

17 Read. Circle *True* or *False*.

Animals Inspire Inventions

Animals move in ways that are unique. People can't swim like dolphins or turn their heads around like owls. Scientists are using computer technology to study the movement of animals. Then they use this knowledge to create interesting inventions that help people.

Elephant-Inspired Arm and Hand

Engineers in England studied the elephant's trunk. They wanted to create a robotic arm and hand that could move just like an arm and could work safely with humans in factories and other places. They created a bionic handling assistant. The assistant looks like an elephant's trunk with a claw. The trunk is very light and very safe. When it accidentally hits a human, it moves back. It is also very gentle. It can pick up an egg!

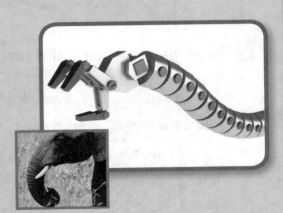

Kingfisher-Inspired Train

A Japanese engineer, Eiji Nakatsu, wanted to solve a problem. The fastest trains in Japan, the bullet trains, made a very loud noise when they came out of tunnels. Trains also slowed down when they came out of tunnels. Eiji loved birds, and he knew that kingfishers dive into the water from the air with no splash. This is because of the shape of their beaks. He worked to change the front of the trains to be more like a kingfisher beak. The problem was solved.

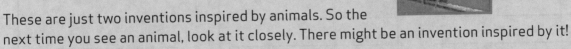

These are just two inventions inspired by animals. So the next time you see an animal, look at it closely. There might be an invention inspired by it!

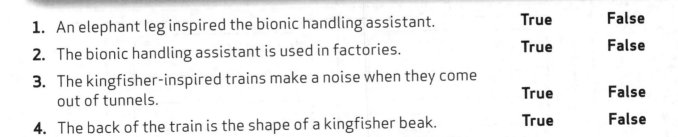

1. An elephant leg inspired the bionic handling assistant. **True**   **False**
2. The bionic handling assistant is used in factories. **True**   **False**
3. The kingfisher-inspired trains make a noise when they come out of tunnels. **True**   **False**
4. The back of the train is the shape of a kingfisher beak. **True**   **False**

18 Which invention in 17 do you think is the most interesting? Why? Write your answer.

_____

_____

When you write a description of an object, it is good to write about:

- The way it looks (**It's** red and large and round. **It looks like** an elephant's trunk.)
- The things it has and can do (**It has** two legs. **It can** go very fast.)
- What it is used for (**It is used to** carry heavy things.)

Include as much information as you can so the readers can see a picture of that object in their mind.

19 Read the paragraph of this cool object. What is it?

This object is really cool. It's rectangular. It has a black or white back. It looks like a thin book, but you can't open or close it. You can carry it everywhere in your bag. You can read and listen to music on it. You can also take pictures and send and receive emails with it. It is used to entertain people on long trips. It's a

_____.

20 Underline the sentences in 19 that describe the way the object looks. Circle the sentences that describe the things it has. Underline twice the things it is used for.

21 Think of an invention. Complete the idea web.

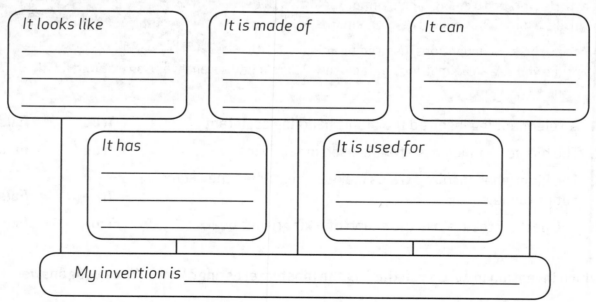

It looks like
_____
_____
_____

It is made of
_____
_____
_____

It can
_____
_____
_____

It has
_____
_____
_____

It is used for
_____
_____
_____

My invention is _____

22 Write a description of an invention. Use 19, 20, and 21 to help you.

23 Look at the code. Write the words. Then match the words and pictures. Write the number.

●	▲	■	▬	◆	◈	⟁	⌄	➢	◁	=	+	÷
a	b	c	d	e	f	g	h	i	j	k	l	m

✕	O	◇	□	▭	✱	!	]	?	#	%	▼	◣
n	o	p	q	r	s	t	u	v	w	x	y	z

1. ⌄ ● ✕ ▬ ✱ - ◈ ▭ ◆ ◆   ◆ ● ▭   ◇ ➢ ◆ ■ ◆

   <u>h</u> _ _ _ _ _ _ _ _ _ _ _ _ _ _ _ _

2. ➢ ✕ ✱ ! ● ✕ !   ■ ● ÷ ◆ □ ●   a. ___

   _ _ _ _ _ _ _ _ _ _ _ _ _

3. ! □ ● ✕ ✱ ➢ ✱ ! O □   □ ● ▬ ➢ O   b. ___

   _ _ _ _ _ _ _ _ _ _ _ _ _ _ _

   c. ___

24 Imagine it's the year 2023. How will you talk about these things? Write the questions. Complete the answers. Use *used to* and *used for* and the words in the box.

> keeping shoes on   play fun games   telling the time   listen to music

1. **A:** These are <u>earphones</u> _____.
   B: <u>What are they used for?</u> _____
   A: They'<u>re used to listen to music</u> _____.

2. **A:** These are _____.
   B: _____?
   A: They're _____.

3. **A:** This is a _____.
   B: _____?
   A: It's _____.

4. **A:** This is a _____.
   B: _____?
   A: It's _____.

WHERE DO THEY COME FROM?

1 Look at the pictures. Read the name of the inventions that come from these places. Do any surprise you?

Italy: eyeglasses, radio, piano

India: chess, ink, pajamas

Canada: basketball, egg carton, IMAX

United States: Post-it® Note, safety pin, voicemail

2 Circle the inventions that you use or see every day.

basketball	chess	egg carton	eyeglasses
IMAX movie system	ink	pajamas	piano
Post-it® Note	radio	safety pin	voicemail

3 Look at 1 and 2. Where do most of the items that you circled come from?

Most of the products that I use or see were invented in _____.

4 What items that you use every day were invented in your country?

_____

5 Read. Circle the **two** correct answers.

1. These are made mostly of metal.

   a. silver earrings **b.** an airplane **c.** a baseball

2. These are made of rubber.

   a. kitchen gloves **b.** T-shirts **c.** rain boots

3. Some of these are made of wool.

   a. candles **b.** blankets **c.** sweaters

4. Some of these are made of cotton.

   a. T-shirts **b.** jackets **c.** tires

5. These are made of clay.

   a. cups **b.** blankets **c.** plates

6 Listen. What are the things? Number them in the order you hear them. Then write the names.

> clothes eraser plate solar-powered car

27
7 Listen and read. Then answer the questions.

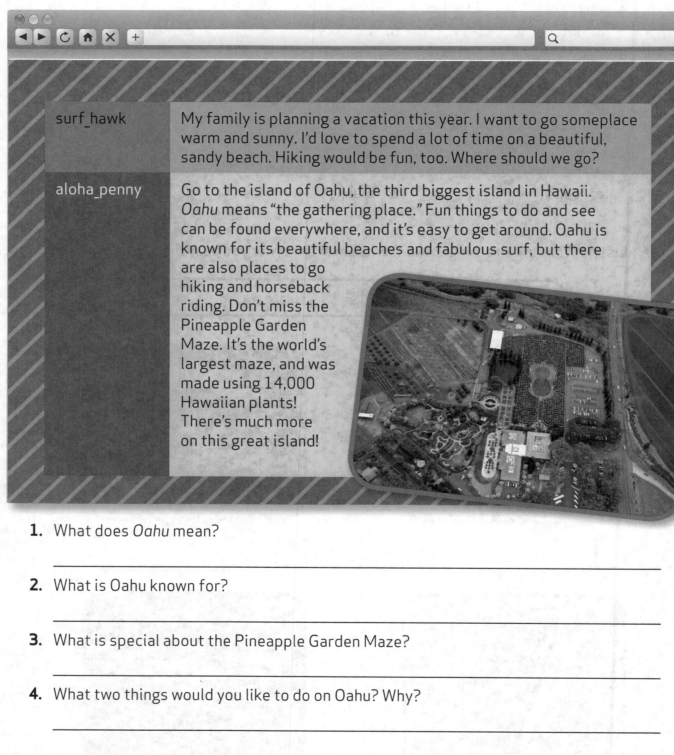

| surf_hawk | My family is planning a vacation this year. I want to go someplace warm and sunny. I'd love to spend a lot of time on a beautiful, sandy beach. Hiking would be fun, too. Where should we go? |
| aloha_penny | Go to the island of Oahu, the third biggest island in Hawaii. *Oahu* means "the gathering place." Fun things to do and see can be found everywhere, and it's easy to get around. Oahu is known for its beautiful beaches and fabulous surf, but there are also places to go hiking and horseback riding. Don't miss the Pineapple Garden Maze. It's the world's largest maze, and was made using 14,000 Hawaiian plants! There's much more on this great island! |

1. What does *Oahu* mean?

   _____

2. What is Oahu known for?

   _____

3. What is special about the Pineapple Garden Maze?

   _____

4. What two things would you like to do on Oahu? Why?

   _____

   _____

8 Listen. Then circle *True* or *False*.

Suzy: Maybe I can find something for my sister here. Her birthday is next week.

Regina: I think you can. That table over there has <u>a bunch of handmade</u> cotton blouses. They're made in Hungary.

Suzy: They're beautiful.

Regina: Look, Margit is wearing one. See how it's worn? The strings are pulled and tied in the front. It's a nice look.

Suzy: My sister would love it! But look, the one that I like is torn.

Regina: I'm sure it can be fixed. Like the sign says, "These are all <u>gently used</u> clothes." Let's ask Margit's mother if it can be repaired.

Suzy: Great idea!

1. It's Suzy's mother's birthday soon.	**True**	**False**
2. Regina likes the blouses.	**True**	**False**
3. Suzy thinks her sister will like the blouse.	**True**	**False**
4. The blouse Suzy likes is new.	**True**	**False**

9 Look at **8**. Read the underlined expressions. Match the expressions with their meaning. Write the letters.

___ **1.** a bunch of

___ **2.** handmade

___ **3.** gently used

a. worn for a little while and still in good condition

b. a lot of

c. made by using your hands and not by using a lot of machines in a factory

10 Complete the sentences with the expressions in **9**.

A: Look at these amazing scarves. Why are they so cheap?

B: I guess it's because they're all ¹_____. But they look new.

A: I'm going to buy the red and yellow one.

B: I love this local craft fair. ²_____ these things look ³_____.

A: I know. I love things that are made by hand.

Grammar

That watch **is made** in Switzerland.
Those bananas **are grown** in Ecuador.

The first pizza **was** probably **made** in Italy.
The first noodles **were** probably **made** in China.

11 Match the three forms of the verbs. Draw lines.

Simple Present	Simple Past	Past Participle
eat	flew	flown
fly	made	invented
grow	ate	raised
introduce	invented	grown
invent	mined	eaten
produce	introduced	made
make	produced	introduced
mine	raised	mined
raise	grew	produced

12 Write the sentences. Use the simple present form of the verb in the passive.

1. Corn _is grown in the United States_____. (grow in United States)

2. Sheep _____. (raise in New Zealand)

3. Many cars _____. (make in China)

4. Gold _____. (mine in South Africa)

5. Denim _____. (produce in many countries)

13 Look. Complete the sentences. Use the simple past of the verb in the passive.

1. Chess _____ probably _____ in India. (invent)

2. In 1783, the first hot air balloon _____. (fly)

3. The first shopping cart _____ in 1937. (make)

4. The phonograph, or record player, _____ in 1877 by Thomas Edison. (introduce)

14 Unscramble the words. Use the words to write sentences. Use the simple present form of the verb in the passive.

1. acrs   rpudeco

   *cars*_____   *produce*_____

   *Cars are produced*_____ in Brazil.

2. ldgo   niem

   _____   _____

   _____ in Peru.

3. sehcs   lypa

   _____   _____

   _____ all over the world.

4. tobos   emda

   _____   _____

   _____ of rubber.

1

1 **Read. Then circle the correct answers.**

Farmers' Markets and Our Future

Farmers all over the world gather on specific days in specific places, like a park or parking lot, to sell their produce directly to customers. Some farmers' markets have live entertainment like singers or musicians and sell things other than produce, like crafts made by local people. They're really fun places.

Shopping at a farmers' market is a good thing to do. Here's why:

1. You can meet local farmers and learn about their produce.

2. Locally grown food tastes good because it's very fresh. Every bite is a treat!

3. The food does not have to travel a long distance from the farm to a distribution center and then to you. It goes only a short distance from the farm to you. This results in less pollution and helps keep the environment clean.

4. Buying from local farmers can help the environment in other ways, too. When farmers do not make enough money to live, they are often obliged to sell their farms to land developers. The developers build houses and buildings on the farmland. More houses may cause more pollution.

5. A typical farm is a beautiful place. It has fields and meadows and woods and ponds. It provides homes to animals like rabbits, birds, and deer. If the farm disappears, the animals may have nowhere to live.

Next time your mom buys produce, think about asking her to go to a local farmers' market. You'll have a fun time.

1. Farmers' markets are always ___.
a. in different places   b. in the same place

2. Buying locally helps the environment because ___.
a. farmers sell the produce cheaply   b. produce travels a short distance from the farm to the market

3. If farmers can't get enough money to live, they might ___.
a. sell their farms   b. build houses

4. If farmers sell their farms, ___.
a. animals will be able to stay on the land   b. some animals will lose their home

16 Read and answer the questions.

Problems and Inventions

Why do people invent things? Where do ideas for inventions come from? There's a saying that "Necessity is the mother of invention." This means that people invent things because there is a problem, and they want to solve the problem.

In 1912 Otto Frederick Rohwedder had an idea. He wanted to invent a machine that could slice a whole loaf of bread. He built his first bread slicer in 1917, but it was destroyed in a fire. In 1927 he had enough money to build another one. But he realized that he had a problem – the bread became stale after it was cut. He then had another idea and he built a bread slicer that sliced the bread and then wrapped it, so that it wouldn't get stale so quickly.

Hacky Sack or Footbag is a fun sport that was invented by John Stalberger and Mike Marshall. In 1972 Mike Marshall made a small beanbag and kicked it in the air with his foot for fun. That same year John Stalberger had knee surgery. His knee exercises after surgery were boring so he looked for a more fun way to exercise. He and Mike shared ideas and the game of Hacky Sack was born.

Society needs inventors. Our lives are better because inventors are problem solvers. Think of a problem. Can you invent something to solve it?

1. What did Otto Frederick Rohwedder invent?

   _____

2. What problem did he have?

   _____

3. How did he solve the problem?

   _____

4. What problem did John Stalberger have?

   _____

5. How did he and Mike Marshall solve this problem?

   _____

When you write a persuasive paragraph, you want your reader to agree with your opinion. A good persuasive paragraph gives a strong main opinion and reasons for that opinion. Your reasons make your opinion stronger and more believable.

Opinion: *Rio de Janeiro is the perfect place to vacation.*

Reasons: *It has beautiful beaches with wonderful swimming and exciting sand sculptures.*

There is a really exciting festival there in February.

It has a famous mountain called Sugar Loaf Mountain. The view from the top is amazing.

17 Read the persuasive paragraph. Then answer the questions.

¹Puerto Vallarta is famous all over the world because it is a wonderful vacation place. It is near the Bay of Banderas in Mexico. ²You won't be bored here because there are a lot of fun things to do. ³You can swim and sunbathe on Playa Los Muertos, a favorite beach, and you can scuba dive here, too. ⁴You can go on walking tours around the old city or boat tours to see dolphins, sea turtles, and humpback whales. ⁵There are forests near Puerto Vallarta where you can see hundreds of colorful birds. You could see a jaguar or an iguana, too. ⁶Puerto Vallarta is full of wonderful adventures for everyone. Visit it on your next vacation.

1. What number sentence is the main opinion? _____

2. How many reasons are given for that opinion? _____

3. What sentence numbers are the reasons? _____

4. Do you want to go there? Why or why not? _____

18 Think of a great vacation spot. Complete the chart with your ideas.

Explain your reason
_____
_____

Name the vacation spot
_____
_____

Give your opinion
_____
_____

Give a second reason
_____
_____

Give a third reason
_____
_____

19 Use your chart in 18. Write a persuasive paragraph about your great vacation spot. Write it on a separate piece of paper.

Vocabulary and Grammar | Review

20 Circle the products that are made of the materials in the chart.

Wool	Rubber	Cotton	Metal	Clay
rug	comb	plate	shopping cart	pottery
scarf	boots	towels	soda can	produce
soda can	paper	jeans	watch	bowls
blanket	eraser	airplane	food	flower pot

21 Read and circle the correct answers.

1. Coffee ___ in Costa Rica and you can visit coffee farms there.

    a. was grown   **b.** is grown

2. Beautiful glass ___ in Italy. You can buy it in fancy stores.

    a. was made   **b.** is made

3. Bar codes ___ in the United States long ago.

    a. were invented   **b.** are invented

4. Fantastic watches ___ in Switzerland and stores all over the world sell them.

    a. are made   **b.** were made

5. A lot of cattle ___ in Argentina today.

    a. were raised   **b.** are raised

6. The jigsaw puzzle ___ by an Englishman in 1767.

    a. was invented   **b.** is invented

22 Complete the sentences with the correct form of the verb.

1. Jars _____ from glass. (make)

2. Apples _____ in New York State and are very popular in the fall. (grow)

3. The modern safety pin _____ in the United States in 1849. (invent)

4. The earliest noodles _____ in China a long, long time ago. (eat)

HOW ADVENTUROUS ARE YOU?

29

1 Listen and read about the food in the pictures. Rate them 1 = I really want to try it! 2 = I might want to try it. 3 = I never want to try it! Write your rating in the box on the pictures.

1. Haggis is a traditional food from Scotland. It is made of chopped sheep liver, heart, and lung. The meat is cooked with oatmeal, onion, and spices. It's pretty spicy, and a little sour.

2. Lamb korma is a traditional dish from India. It is made with lamb, yogurt, and spices like pepper and curry. Sometimes a creamy coconut milk sauce is used instead of yogurt.

3. Eskimo ice cream comes from Alaska. It has a very different taste from ice cream you might know. It is made with reindeer fat and berries. And no sugar is added to it.

4. Tamagoyaki comes from Japan. It is made of eggs, soy sauce, sugar, and fish seasoning. It tastes a little sweet and a little fishy.

5. Poutine is a dish from Quebec, Canada. It is a special kind of French fries. The fries are topped with gravy and cheese.

6. Red bean cakes, called *mochi*, are a popular dessert and sweet snack in Japan. They are made of mashed beans and sugar.

2 Look at your ratings. How adventurous with food are you? Check (✓) your answer.

- [ ] I'm very adventurous. I rated most of the pictures a **1.**
- [ ] I'm a little adventurous. I rated most of the pictures a **2.**
- [ ] I'm not adventurous at all. I rated most of the pictures a **3.**

3 Listen. Check the words you hear for each food.

		unusual	tasty	popular	raw	spicy	sweet	sour	traditional	delicious
1.	guacamole									
2.	babotie									
3.	kimchi									
4.	sashimi									
5.	sweet and sour chicken									
6.	chocolate-covered grasshoppers									

4 What food do you like? What food don't you like? What does it taste like?

_____

_____

5 Listen and read. Then answer the questions.

LIFE ON a BOAT

Eleven-year-old Glenn Dodd has lived on a boat with his family for the past two years. A local radio station is interviewing him.

Michael Dean: Today we're talking to 11-year-old Glenn Dodd on *Awesome Adventures*. Glenn's family has lived on a boat and has traveled around Australia for the last two years. Tell me, Glenn, what's it like living on a boat?

Glenn Dodd: Well, in the beginning it was really hard. There are four people in my family, and a dog. The boat is small, so we were always very close to each other.

Michael Dean: Wow! I bet that was tough sometimes.

Glenn Dodd: Yeah, we had to learn to get along, or my dad said he'd throw us into the sea!

Michael Dean: That would make me behave, too! What do you like the most about life on a boat?

Glenn Dodd: Well, probably all the new things I can try.

Michael Dean: Like what? Give me an example.

Glenn Dodd: Well, I've eaten crocodile meat a few times. And I've snorkeled with stingrays. That was a little scary!

Michael Dean: I bet! Tell me, after two years, would you rather live on a boat or live in a house?

Glenn Dodd: Honestly, I really want to be in a house now, like my friends. Actually, my family has decided to go back home next month. So, soon, I'm going to be a land creature.

Michael Dean: Well, good luck. That's all the time we have. Thanks again, Glenn, for sharing your story.

1. Where does Glenn Dodd live now? _____

2. What does Glenn like most about living there? _____
3. Do you think Glenn is an adventurous person? Why or why not? _____

6 Listen. Then circle the correct answers.

Allie: Hey, Roberto. Let's <u>do something</u> on Saturday afternoon.

Roberto: <u>That sounds good</u>, Allie. But I have a class on Saturday.

Allie: You have school on Saturday?

Roberto: Yeah. I'm learning Chinese!

Allie: Chinese? Really?

Roberto: Yeah. It's really cool. Have you ever studied another language?

Allie: Well, I can speak English and Spanish. But I've never studied another language.

Roberto: It's a lot of fun. And I'm learning a lot. I can say so many things in Chinese already.

Allie: <u>That's cool</u>! How do you say *hello* in Chinese?

Roberto: Ni hao, Allie!

Allie: Hola, Roberto!

1. Roberto and Allie are   **a.** friends.   **b.** brother and sister.

2. Roberto studies Chinese on   **a.** Sundays.   **b.** Saturdays.

3. Allie speaks   **a.** English and Chinese.   **b.** English and Spanish.

4. Roberto   **a.** enjoys studying Chinese.   **b.** doesn't like studying Chinese.

5. Ni hao means   **a.** good-bye.   **b.** hello.

7 Look at 6. Read the underlined expressions. How can you say them in other words? Match and write the letter.

___ 1. do something   **a.** Wow! That's great!

___ 2. That sounds good.   **b.** Let's go somewhere and have fun.

___ 3. That's cool!   **c.** That's a good idea.

8 Complete the sentences with the expressions in 7.

A: Hi, Jack. Do you want to [1]_____ on Sunday afternoon?

B: [2]_____. Do you want to go to a movie? I have two tickets, and they were free!

A: [3]_____. How did you get them?

B: They were a gift.

Grammar

Have you ever **been** to a concert?	Yes, I **have**./No, I **haven't**.
Has he ever **been** skydiving?	Yes, he **has**./No, he **hasn't**.

9 Match the three forms of the verbs. Draw lines.

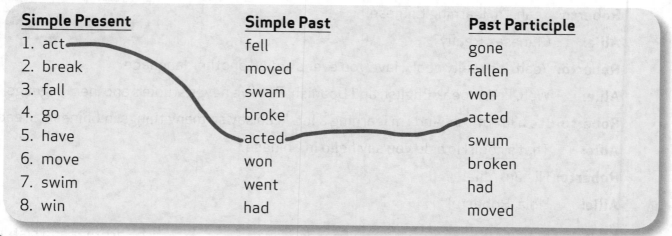

Simple Present	Simple Past	Past Participle
1. act	fell	gone
2. break	moved	fallen
3. fall	swam	won
4. go	broke	acted
5. have	acted	swum
6. move	won	broken
7. swim	went	had
8. win	had	moved

10 Unscramble the questions. Then look and write the answers.

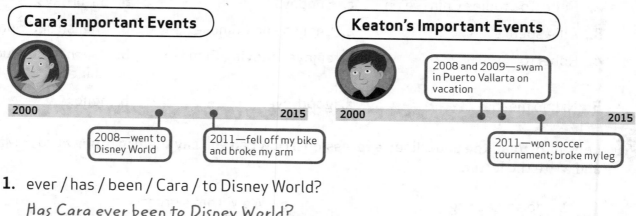

Cara's Important Events

2000 — 2015

2008—went to Disney World

2011—fell off my bike and broke my arm

Keaton's Important Events

2008 and 2009—swam in Puerto Vallarta on vacation

2000 — 2015

2011—won soccer tournament; broke my leg

1. ever / has / been / Cara / to Disney World?

   Has Cara ever been to Disney World?

   Yes, she has.

2. Cara / swum / ever / has / in Puerta Vallarta?

   _____

   _____

3. Keaton / has / gone / to Puerta Vallarta / ever?

   _____

   _____

4. Keaton / broken / his arm / has / ever?

   _____

   _____

Would they rather play soccer or watch it?	They'd rather play soccer.

I'd = I would
you'd = you would
he'd = he would
she'd = she would
they'd = they would

11 Follow the lines. Make guesses and answer the questions.

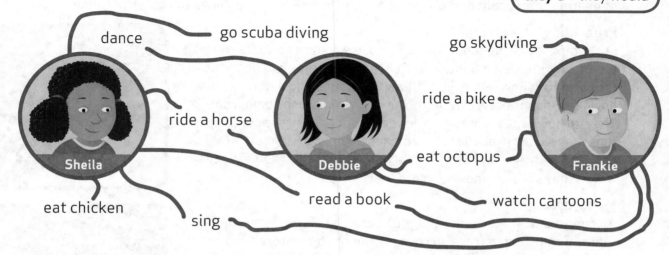

1. Would Sheila rather go skydiving or go scuba diving?

   She'd rather go scuba diving.

2. Would Sheila and Debbie rather ride a bike or ride a horse?

   _____

3. Would Frankie rather eat chicken or eat octopus?

   _____

4. Would Frankie and Sheila rather watch cartoons or read a book?

   _____

12 Answer the questions.

1. Would you rather eat chicken or eat octopus?

   _____

2. Would you rather ride a bike or ride a horse?

   _____

3. Would you rather go skydiving or go scuba diving?

   _____

13 Read. Then circle *True* or *False*.

Extreme Sports

Some people love the feel of adrenaline rushing through their bodies, giving them that extra boost of energy. This is called an adrenaline rush. People do many things to feel an adrenaline rush.

Freeriding

Freeriding is like big-wave surfing on snow. Skiers go to the very top of a high, steep mountain and ski down it. There are no paths for them to follow—they just follow the slopes and natural paths down the mountain. Where does the adrenaline rush come from? They go down the mountain very, very fast because the slopes that they ski down are very steep. Some slopes are almost at 90 degrees to the ground. They also fly high in the air in some places where they ski over snow-covered rock cliffs.

Motorcycle racing

All over the world there are people who enjoy motorcycle riding. Some people travel across continents on motorcycles because they find it fun and it relieves stress. But others are not interested in relaxing—they want an adrenaline rush, so they race motorcycles at very high speeds. They ride around a track, and on the straight part of the track they can go up to 200 miles per hour. When they go around a corner they lean over so that their knees nearly touch the ground, and they sometimes do that at about 130 miles per hour. That's fast!

1. Freeriders ski down very high and steep mountains.   **True**   **False**

2. Motorcycle racers can go faster round corners than on the straight part of the track.   **True**   **False**

3. Freeriders and motorcycle racers want an adrenaline rush.   **True**   **False**

4. Freeriders and motorcycle racers aren't adventurous.   **True**   **False**

5. Freeriders follow a path.   **True**   **False**

14 Answer the question.

Which of these sports would you like to watch? Why?

_____

_____

15 **Read. Then answer the questions.**

Record-breaking Kids

Jordan Romero is an amazing teenager who has climbed seven of the highest and most challenging mountains on seven continents. He climbed his first mountain, Mt. Kilimanjaro in Africa, in 2006 when he was 10. He's the youngest person in the world to do this. In 2011, when he was 15, he climbed the last of the seven mountains, a mountain in Antarctica. Jordan, who lives in California, wants to help other kids reach their goals, so he started a group called *Find Your Everest*.

In 2012 a Dutch teenager, Laura Dekker, became the youngest person to sail around the world on her own. Laura has been on or near water all her life. She was born on a boat, got her first boat when she was six, and at age eight began dreaming about sailing around the world. At 10 she got her second boat, *Guppy*, and at 15 she set off on her long trip. A year and a day later, she achieved her goal. She was just 16 years old. When Laura finished the trip and got off her boat, her mother, father, sister, grandparents, and many cheering fans greeted her.

1. How many mountains on how many continents has Jordan Romero climbed?

   _____

2. How old was he when he climbed his last mountain?

   _____

3. What does *Find Your Everest* do?

   _____

4. How old was Laura when she got her first boat?

   _____

5. How old was she when she set off to achieve her goal?

   _____

6. At 16, what record did Laura set?

   _____

16 **Answer the question.**

Pretend that you could interview one of these kids. Which one would you interview? What two questions would you ask?

_____

_____

A good description includes:

- a clear topic sentence that tells the reader what you are going to write about. Example: *I'm not a risk taker.*
- more information about the topic that gives examples or details. You can introduce your examples using *For example.* Notice the comma after the words. *For example, I don't like to try new foods. I get nervous when I go to new places where I can't speak the language.*
- a summary that retells your topic sentence in a new way. Example: *It's OK that I'm not a risk taker because it's good to have different people in the world.*

17 Read the description. Then answer the questions. Write the numbers.

> ¹I'm not at all adventurous, and I don't like to try new things. ²For example, I don't play sports because every time I've played, I've gotten hurt. ³I also don't like trying new foods, and I prefer to eat the same food every day. ⁴This is strange because my whole family loves trying food from different cultures. ⁵Everyone says I should be more adventurous and try new things, but I'm happy just the way I am.

_____ **1.** What sentence is the topic sentence?

_____ **2.** What sentences give details about the topic?

_____ **3.** What sentence retells the topic in a new way?

18 Think of ways that you are *not* adventurous. Complete the chart.

Complete the sentence: I am not adventurous because
Give an example and details.
Give another example and details.
Write a summary. Explain in one sentence how you are not adventurous.

19 Write a paragraph about how you are *not* adventurous. Use **18** to help you. Write on a separate piece of paper.

20 **Find and circle these words.**

```
        q z i w
      a x c b w j t k
    n o m v d q y r f d
    u d p z p a r a w s
  a n s o u r g h d i a m
  i u m p m r s p i c y n
  l s f u b l w g t p z b
  q u p l x y e f i j n v
  a a e a g l e d o t e c
  l q r w q t s n y u s
      t a s t y a a s y
        i m v l j l
```

popular
raw
sour
spicy
sweet
tasty
traditional
unusual

21 **Complete the sentences. Use some of the words in 20.**

1. One soup at the Spanish restaurant has a lot of spices in it. Not many people order it.

    The soup is too _____ so it isn't _____.

2. Many of the dishes at the Greek restaurant are delicious seafood dishes. One of the dishes is eaten by everyone in Greece and was eaten long ago, too.

    That seafood dish is _____ and _____.

3. The new Mexican restaurant has a dessert that is made of avocado and lime.

    The avocado dessert isn't common. It's _____. It isn't sweet like usual desserts. It's _____.

22 **Complete the sentences. Use the correct form of the words in parentheses. Then answer the questions about yourself.**

1. _____ you ever _____ to a Japanese Restaurant? (go)

    _____

2. _____ you ever _____ an octopus? (see)

    _____

3. _____ you ever _____ grasshoppers? (eat)

    _____

Think Big

1 Unscramble and write the words. Add your own word on the extra line.

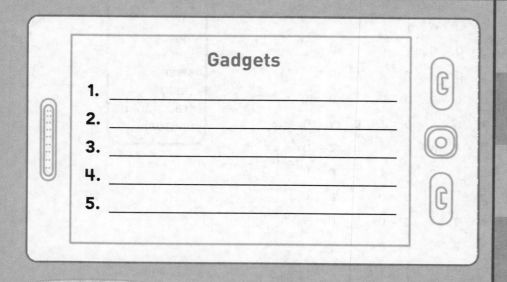

Gadgets

1. _____
2. _____
3. _____
4. _____
5. _____

1. nattisn aecamr

2. optlbrea agem edievc

3. tniasrsort rdaoi

4. ivdoe aemg syetsm

Products and Materials

1. _cotton jeans_____
2. _____
3. _____
4. _____

1. tootnc janes

2. urrbeb botos

3. yacl

1. edusoiilc

2. lpruapo

3. tadiilnroat

4. uusulan

Food

1. _____
2. _____
3. _____
4. _____
5. _____

2 **Find a song that talks about gadgets, products and materials, or food.**
Complete the chart about the song.

Song title	
Who is the singer?	
Where does the singer come from?	
Who was the song written by?	
What is your favorite line in the song? Why is it your favorite?	
Would the singer rather sing traditional songs or popular songs?	
Has the song ever been a number one hit?	
Who else do you think might sing the song well?	

3 **Write a note to your parents. Persuade them to let you go to a concert to hear this song and singer. Use the information in 1 and 2 to help you.**

4 **In Your Classroom**

Work in pairs and share.

1 Read about Lisa and Don. Complete the sentences with the correct words. Use the correct form of the verbs.

Lisa

"I'm in the drama club. I play drums in the school band. I can draw, but I can't paint. Soccer is fun, but baseball is boring."

"I'm in the math club. I want to learn how to do karate. Soccer is fun, but baseball isn't fun. I can't draw."

Don

1. Lisa is good at _____. (draw/paint)
2. Don is interested in _____. (act/learn karate)
3. They aren't interested in _____. (draw/play baseball)
4. They enjoy _____. (play soccer/play baseball)

2 Look at 1. Complete the sentences.

1. Lisa _____. (good at/paint)
2. Don _____. (enjoy/draw)
3. Don _____. (like/do math)
4. Lisa _____. (love/play drums)

3 Look at 1. Complete the sentences with the correct form of the verbs.

1. **Lisa:** How about joining the art club?

   Don: No, thanks. I _____. (like)

2. **Don:** Do you want to join the math club?

   Lisa: I don't think so. I _____. (interested in)

3. **Emily:** How about joining the soccer club?

   Don and Lisa: Cool! We _____. (love)

4. **Brian:** Why don't you try out for the baseball team?

   Don and Lisa: No way! We _____. (enjoy)

1 Complete the sentences. Use the correct form of the verbs.

1.

My parents _____ (get married) when they _____ (be) very young. A few months later, they _____ (move) to Los Angeles.

2.

My father _____ (open) his own restaurant in San Diego when I _____ (be) in my teens. I _____ (work) with my father every weekend. A few years ago, I _____ (help) my father open his second restaurant.

2 Read and draw the picture. Then write the answer.

1. Alice is shorter than Carl. Barbara is taller than Alice, but shorter than Carl.

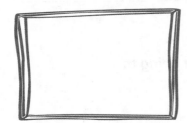

Who is the tallest?

_____

2. Jose is younger than Frank. Frank is older than Edward. Edward is older than Jose.

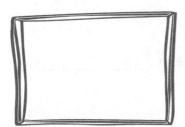

Who is the youngest?

_____

3. My brother, Ted, is very strong. He's stronger than my dad. My dad is stronger than my mom. I'm Mark. I'm stronger than Ted.

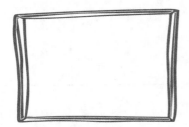

Who is the strongest in the family?

_____

1 How could students help their school? Make suggestions. Use *could* and the words in the box.

> clean up the pond   paint the art room   plant flowers

1.

Sophia _____

_____

2.

Brandon _____

_____

3.

Jillian _____

_____

2 Unscramble the words. Then write sentences with *is/am/are going to*.

What are these students going to do this week?

1. shaw arsc

_____

We _____

2. rweti alteircs

_____

Peter and Jake _____

3. atek iputrsce

_____

I _____

4. eakm sptrseo

_____

Rebekah _____

1 Look at the chart. Complete the sentences. Use *more/less ... than* and *the least/the most.*

	Jeff	Tony	Silvia
Making a Volcano	👍👍	👍👍	👍
Mixing oil and water	👍	👍	👍👍
Making Electricity	👍👍👍	👍👍	👍👍👍

How did the students feel about their science class experiments?

1. **Silvia:** Mixing liquids was _____ making a volcano. (interesting)

2. **Jeff:** Making electricity was _____ of all. (exciting)

3. **Tony:** Mixing liquids was _____ experiment. (amazing)

4. **Jeff:** Making a volcano was _____ making electricity. (challenging)

2 Look at 1. Write sentences. Use *as ... as* and *not as ... as.*

1. **Jeff:** Making a volcano / fun / making electricity.

   Making a volcano is not as fun as making electricity.

2. **Tony:** Making electricity / exciting / making a volcano.

   _____

3. **Silvia:** Mixing liquids / interesting / making electricity.

   _____

3 Look at 1. Write sentences. Use *too* and *not enough* and the words in parentheses.

1. **Silvia:** I didn't like making a volcano. It was _____. (interesting)

2. **Jeff:** Mixing liquids wasn't cool. It was _____. (boring)

3. **Tony:** I'm not interested in mixing liquids. It was _____. (exciting)

1 Match the puzzle pieces. Then complete the story. Use the sentences on the puzzle pieces and the correct form of the verbs.

Charlie's Silly Dream

Puzzle pieces:
- She / turn the pancakes
- Charlie / fall asleep
- his math book / sing him songs
- Charlie / walk to school
- Charlie / have a snack
- his backpack / began to fly
- The bananas / jog on the table
- the pancakes / start dancing

In the morning

Charlie's mother was making pancakes for breakfast.

¹_She was turning the pancakes_ when _the pancakes started dancing._

"Time for school, Charlie," said his mom.

² _____ when _____.

In the afternoon

Charlie was hungry.

³ _____ while _____.

At night

Charlie was doing his math homework. Then he got very tired.

⁴ _____ while _____.

His soccer ball turned off the light. "Good night, Charlie."

2 Circle the correct answers.

1. What was Charlie doing when his backpack began to fly?

   a. He was walking to school.   **b.** He walked to school.

2. What was his mom doing when the pancakes started dancing?

   a. She was making breakfast.   **b.** She made breakfast.

3. Was Charlie jogging when he had a snack?

   a. No, he didn't.   **b.** No, he wasn't.

4. Was he sleeping when the soccer ball turned out the light?

   a. Yes, he was.   **b.** Yes, he did.

1 Read. Then complete the sentences. Use *no one* and *everyone*.

One hundred years
from now . . .

In 100 years the world will be very different. ¹_____ will use
smartphones because our phone will be inside our head! ²_____
will use flying cars, not gas cars, and ³_____ will live in
apartments in tall buildings in space. Not like today. Today many people
live in houses. In the future, ⁴_____ will live in houses anymore.
Machines will make our food at home and in restaurants. ⁵_____
will need to cook anymore. ⁶_____ will study in schools
because there won't be any school buildings, and we won't have teachers.
⁷_____ will study at home using computers.

2 Look at 1. Complete the sentences. Use *will* or *won't*.

1. There _____ any teachers. (be)

2. We _____ people with cell phones. (call)

3. We _____ in apartments in space. (live)

4. People _____ flying cars. (drive)

5. We _____. (cook) Machines _____ (cook)
   for us.

3 Match the sentences. Write the letters.

In the future . . .

___ 1. Students won't need teachers.

___ 2. We'll go to the moon on vacation.

___ 3. No one will go to friends' houses.

___ 4. Everyone will be happy.

a. We'll meet by video messaging.

b. They'll teach themselves.

c. Nobody will be sad.

d. Spaceship travel will be cheap.

4 Look at 3. Do you think these things will happen? Write your answers.

1. *Students will teach themselves some things, but they will need teachers, too.*

2. _____

3. _____

1 Complete the sentences. Use *is/are used to* and words from the box.

> eat   get around   protect eyes   write

1. A pencil _____.
2. Plates _____.
3. A bike _____.
4. Sunglasses _____.

2 What do you think these are? Write sentences. Use *It may be* or *It might be.*

1.

_____

2.

_____

3.

_____

4.

_____

3 Answer the questions. Use the words in parentheses.

1. I'm thinking of something. It's round and hard. People play a fun game with it. What do you think it is?

   _____. (may)

2. I'm thinking of a kind of sweet food. They're small and taste great. They're great at birthday parties. What do you think they are?

   _____. (might)

3. I'm thinking of a small insect. It likes hot, wet weather. It can fly, and it makes a noise when it flies. What do you think it is?

   _____. (might)

1 Complete the sentences. Use the correct passive form of the verb.

1. The very first cookie ___was invented___ around the 7th century in Persia. (invent)

2. Crops, such as rice and corn, _____ in many countries today. (raise)

3. In 2005 a bowl of noodles four thousand years old _____ by scientists in China. (discover)

4. Delicious oranges _____ in Florida every year. (grow)

5. A lot of coffee _____ in Colombia these days. (produce)

2 Complete the puzzle. Write the letters. Use the words in the box.

Africa	Argentina	Brazil	China
invent	mine	produce	raise

1.	2.	3.	4.
A f r **d i a m o n d s** c a	A r **c a t t l e** _ _ _ _	C _ _ **n o o d l e s** _ _ _	i _ B **r u b b e r** _ _ _ _ _ m _

3 Look at 2. Write sentences. Use *is/are* or *was/were* and the words in the puzzle.

1. _Diamonds are mined in Africa._

2. _____

3. _____

4. _____

1 Look at the chart. Complete and answer the questions.

	fly to the USA	win a spelling bee	ride a horse	visit Chile	eat octopus
Gloria	✓			✓	✓
Rod		✓	✓		✓

1. _____Has_____ Gloria ever _____flown_____ to the USA?

   _Yes, she has._____

2. _____ Gloria ever _____ a spelling bee?

   _____

3. _____ Gloria ever _____ Chile?

   _____

4. _____ Rod ever _____ octopus?

   _____

5. _____ Rod ever _____ a horse?

   _____

Gloria

Rod

2 Read. Then complete and answer the questions.

> Tom and Sara like spicy food, adventurous sports, beaches, and adrenaline rushes. Karen likes unusual food, but she doesn't like hot spices, scary sports, mountains, or adrenaline rushes.

1. _____Would_____ Karen _____rather_____ eat spicy food or chocolate-covered grasshoppers?

   _She'd rather eat chocolate-covered grasshoppers._____

2. _____ Tom and Sara _____ visit a museum or ski down a mountain?

   _____

3. _____ Sara _____ go swimming or mountain climbing?

   _____

4. _____ Tom and Sara _____ ride a motorcycle fast or slowly?

   _____

5. _____ Karen _____ ski fast down a mountain or walk in the woods?

   _____

Workbook 5

My BIG ENGLISH World

1 **Make your own My Big English World book.**

1. Fold a piece of paper in half and make a 4-page book.

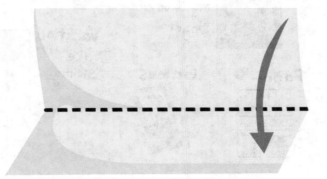

2. Make your own My Big English World book cover. Draw or paste your picture on your cover. Write your name.

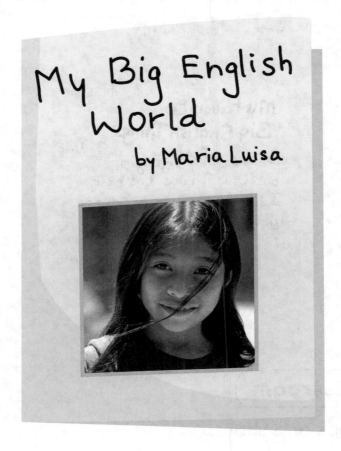

3. Look and listen around you every day. Open your My Big English World book. Write the title *English Around Me*. Draw, write, and paste things you see and hear in English. Write names, words, and sentences.

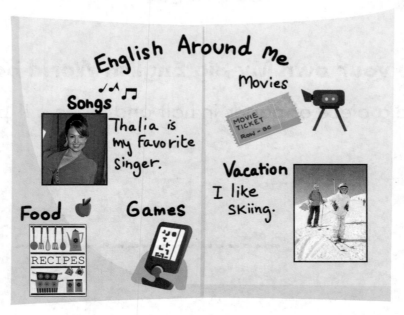

4. Close your book and make a back cover. Draw or write about your favorite things in Big English.

In Your Classroom

Work in groups and share.